Also available by Camouflaged Sisters

Camouflaged Sisters:
*Revealing Struggles of the Black Woman's
Military Experience*

Camouflaged Sisters:
Silent No More

Camouflaged Sisters Presents:
Behind the Rank, Volume 1

Camouflaged Sisters Presents:
Behind the Rank, Volume 2

Camouflaged Sisters:
*Leadership Through the Eyes of Senior
Military Women Leaders*

BEHIND THE
RANK

VOL 3

BEHIND THE
RANK

VOL 3

LILA HOLLEY

purposely
created
PUBLISHING

BEHIND THE RANK, VOL 3
Published by Purposely Created Publishing Group™
Copyright © 2019 Lila Holley

All rights reserved.

Printed in the United States of America

ISBN: 978-1-64484-084-9

Special discounts are available on bulk quantity purchases by book clubs, associations and special interest groups. For details email: sales@publishyourgift.com or call (888) 949-6228.

For information logon to: www.PublishYourGift.com

TABLE OF CONTENTS

STRENGTH TO SERVE

FOREWORD

"Woman must not accept; she must challenge.
She must not be awed by that which has been built up
around her; she must reverence that woman in her
which struggles for expression."

—Margaret Sanger

These powerful words from Margaret Sanger embody the vision Lila Holley expresses within her books. It has taken me many lessons, experiences, and trials to get to the point where I could allow myself to be free to express and share my voice. Lila understands this journey. When Lila asked me if I'd be willing to write a foreword for her book, knowing her character and level of professionalism, that was enough for me to say yes.

I feel like I've known Lila for a long time. We both share an unlikely road to success from humble origins. Both from the great state of New York, facing challenges while making and walking into a decision that changed the trajectory of our lives... joining the United States Army. Lila and I connected through Facebook when I reached out to her after purchasing her book *Camouflaged Sisters: Revealing Struggles of the Black Woman's Military Experience*, which I found empowering. A few years later, we met during her visit to the Midwest, where she keynoted the Fort Leavenworth Equal Opportunity Office Women's History Month program. The rest is history! Lila has a spirited, energetic, and authentic way of empowering women Veterans to action. Her impact is evident in the manifestation of several multiple award-winning, Amazon bestselling books where her selfless spirit and endless mission is to partner with and empower military women and women Veterans to share their stories. This is exemplary of what leaders do. Although she is now a retiree and Veteran, she continues to use the same tools of military leadership to influence others to accomplish the mission by providing purpose, direction, and motivation. That level of dedication is deeply embedded and shall not cease with CW4 (Retired) Holley.

The stories shared in this book are those that many military women can relate to. Each page affirms my story, your story, and the overall importance of having our voices heard in a world that continues to view us as invisible.

In my book *Jewels of Wisdom*, I wrote a quote titled "Lessons." I'd like to offer up this quote to Camouflaged Sisters readers who will understand what it means to have lived the experience of "duty to serve."

I am now fully convinced that the path we tread are meant to be full of lessons learned, good and bad, overcoming challenges, building strength and embracing the beauty of the warrior that rises above it all. Somebody needs you!

Behind the Rank, Volume 3, is a movement that continues to evolve. I am proud to be on the front lines alongside Lila and in solidarity with all of you.

Dr. Estacy Porter
CPT (Retired), US Army
Editor-in-Chief, *Voices of Virtuous Veterans Magazine*,
Co-author of *Wholistic Women Win* and author of *Jewels of Wisdom*

INTRODUCTION

They say the third time is a charm! Well, we're back and we couldn't agree more!

In *Behind the Rank, Volume 1*, we shared stories from 29 courageous military women that focused on: Duty to Self, Duty to Serve, and Duty to Family. In *Behind the Rank, Volume 2*, we dug a little deeper into Duty to Self and 17 authors shared how they were able to take the wounds of life and go through a healing process to now look at their life scars as a sign of beauty.

In *Behind the Rank, Volume 3*, we bring you more intimate stories from 19 courageous military women, allowing our readers to learn even more about the plight of women serving in the military. As always, we share our stories in hopes of leaving our readers inspired by our transparency. We write to our sisters-in-arms to both motivate and remind them that they are not alone in their plight to be understood and accepted. I always say that the story of the military woman is layered—the good, the not so good, and the downright ugly. Camouflaged Sisters books allow you to look at all layers of our stories, in our own voices, as military women—always honoring our service.

In this book, we dig deeper into Duty to Serve...

Journey with us as we go further *Behind the Rank*, understanding the military woman's Duty to Serve. The word duty means an obligation or action someone is required to perform. While many military women, to include the women in this book, join and serve in the military for numerous reasons, many maintain that their Duty to Serve had and continues to have more to do with their ability to serve as women. Many military women will say they are proud of surviving a military career—the physical and mental demands of training and the stress of the job. Many are proud to tell about what they survived.

Then there are the many who still can't share that they served because of the pain they endured during their military careers. Whether they endured the traumatic pain of being violated due to a military sexual assault or they fought the painful and exhausting battle of having to prove themselves day after day during their career, most women will admit that they equate a level of pain with their military careers.

Our obligation with the Camouflaged Sisters brand, books, and movement is to first, value the voice of military women and second, honor their service. For so long, many military women felt that they did not have a voice or that their stories did not matter. Many fight the feeling of being the "invisible Veteran" after their service. Diving deeper into Duty to Serve is our way of giving value to their voices and honor to their service. As a woman Veteran myself, I believe that military women are indeed a unique breed of women who now belong to a special sisterhood. As these courageous women share their stories about their journey, many will learn that there are two types of women who join and serve in the military:

- ❯ Running towards... The woman who joins the military because she is running towards validation, acceptance, or a desire to be a part of something bigger. Oftentimes, these are the women who join the military to provide for their family.

- ❯ Running from... The woman who joins the military because she is running from something is often running from her life situation and looking to recreate or find herself. Oftentimes, these are the women who join the military to get away from their family.

I would say I was definitely running towards something when I joined the military. I was a teenage mother and needed a way to provide for my son and contribute financially to my family. I guess I also had a little of the second type of woman in me as well because as my career progressed, I felt like I recreated myself or maybe I just unleashed the leader that resided in me all along but was never in an environment to grow. And if I can be honest, I did feel the need to run away from my situations—failed relationships, a sorry attempt at college life, low paying jobs, and uncertainty about where my life was headed. The Army allowed me to focus and grow the leader within. It also gave me hope about my future. I still had a lot of growing to do because I went in with a lot of mental baggage. But, over time I reshaped my mindset and had a successful career.

As you read these stories, you will see that these women had to deal with many obstacles in their lives and careers—whether they were running towards validation or running from a life worth leaving behind to create a new one. Above everything they faced, their Duty to Serve remained strong and became the driving force for them to endure any pain they encountered along their journey. Whether it was their service to their families, their Troops, their country, or themselves, they stayed dedicated to their duty. In many cases, all they had was their faith to push them through, yet they remained positive and shining examples of leaders dedicated to their Duty to Serve.

Lila H.

FAITH TO SERVE

STRENGTH TO CARRY ON

☆ ☆ ☆ ☆ ☆

CHARLOTTE CARROLL

Traumatic Brain Injury

I had a concussion in 2006 which developed into traumatic brain injury (TBI) while serving on Active Duty. We were doing some intense hand-to-hand combat training, which included choke outs. If you've never been choked out, it is when air is stopped from going to your brain and your body goes limp. In the police academy this is simulated, but not in the Army. I have to say that I loved it until the damage was done. Now because of the damage done to my brain, I am required to have MRIs regularly. These MRIs note the injuries to my brain to include brain vascular malformation and Chiari I malformation, both affecting many parts of my brain. These injuries result in memory problems, behavioral problems, anger issues, and major headaches. I also have issues with my vision and balance problems, which have resulted in me falling several times in my house. I also suffer with stomach issues and vomit in my sleep. Now I must be watched when I sleep because oftentimes I wake up choking. When I am able to sleep, it is normally with the help of medication because the pain in my body is so bad it is hard to sleep.

I must admit that I am a danger to my family and myself, having set off the smoke detectors and started a fire on several occasions. I can no longer prepare meals because I forget the food on the stove. The stress is overwhelming and at times I feel so hopeless and helpless. This stress has sometimes required visits to the psych hospital.

In addition to all of that, I also suffer from PTSD (post-traumatic stress disorder). At times, I don't know if it is the PTSD that came from military sexual trauma (MST) or the TBI that makes me feel hopeless and depressed.

My struggles are real, yet I am learning to deal with life. I will be honest, it has been a challenge. I love to work out and get physical but that had to change. No more running, so I walk. But along with that came knee problems, making it hard to walk. There have been times when I wanted to give up and not live anymore, but it is my faith that keeps me holding on. I had to ask for help, and now I understand that asking for help is ok.

It is hard to understand these conditions and how they work on one's ability to think and move forward. When faced with any type of challenge, it is important to take your time and learn to live where you are. Letting go of the anger took a great deal of time for me. I still get lost in my feelings and can sometimes go to a very dark place. It takes a lot of training and help from mental health experts to get moving and back into the light.

Faith to Carry On

I want my story to help you, letting you know that things can and will get better. Keep the faith and trust God. I make an effort to pray daily, sometimes 40 times a day. I need God in my life because with Him I can do all things. I truly believe that. So, I am reaching out to let you know that whatever you are going through will pass. Life will get better. It is important to keep your faith in God and surround yourself with Godly people who will lift you up, not bring you down. We can't make a temporary event a permanent event. Every year I like to take inventory of the people in my life—the ones that should stay and the ones that need to go. It is ok to let people go because they were in your life for that season. Everyone can't go where God is taking you, so it is okay to say bye.

Keep your focus on God and He will open doors that man can't close. Believe in yourself and do not let negative words define who you are. That includes self-talk, so be mindful of what you say to yourself daily. Once you eliminate the negative people, you will see a difference in your life and how you feel about yourself will improve. I have to thank God for all the blessings that He has given me, all the battles He has helped me fight, and for never leaving me alone to face my life's challenges by myself.

Injured but Not Broken

Life as I knew it had changed. It had changed in a way that I can't say I liked, but I learned to adapt and overcome. When people look at me, they don't understand the battle that I face daily. When your injuries are internal not external, they can't be seen with the naked eye. The battle that I have every second, every minute, and every hour is within my mind. I have learned that it is ok to ask for help when I need help, it is not a sign of weakness but a sign of strength. Our hardest battles are in the mind, some are real and some are not.

Faith is something I depend and lean on to help me. I also keep positive and strong people around me. My greatest challenge is my memory. I can put something down and it will take hours to find the document that I just had in my hand. I am telling you to manage your anger, but I had to practice this over and over so I wouldn't get angry because I couldn't remember something. That makes things worse. My thought process is slower than normal. It takes longer for me to comprehend what is being said, which affects my attention span and ability to concentrate. The headaches can take me out for days and weeks sometimes. I deal with weakness and numbness in all my limbs daily. Emotionally, I fight depression, anxiety, and fear most of the time. It can be very overwhelming.

What do you do when the biggest enemy in your life is *you*? I have been a fighter all my life, but how many of you know that when you have to fight yourself, the battle can get very real. I want to make a positive impact on others and being real is the only way I know how to do that. This is my life; I am injured but not broken. The fear is immobilizing, and sometimes the danger feels like it is greater than anything I have had to deal with before. But sometimes there is nothing there, it is all in my mind.

I had to work on self-love. I heard in one of Whitney Houston songs, "The greatest love of all is happening to me... learning to love yourself, it is the greatest love of all." Love yourself so that it will be easy for you to love others. It does start and end with you and your feelings, but don't forget that feelings change. I had to learn my *why*. Why am I still here? What is my purpose? What should I be doing with my life? And, is God happy with what I am doing? For me it was knowing my *why* and learning to walk in that purpose. I know there is more of my story to come as I make peace with myself, let go of what I once was, and embrace who I am now.

I refuse to walk around in fear, even if the enemy I face is within. I will learn to deal with the present while accepting my past. This will be hard to do, but I must fight that battle.

This is not the life that I would wake up and want to live each day, but it is the life I live now. I do have a decision to make in life. I am choosing to live and be a better person. I am not my disability, but I am disabled. And though there is nothing wrong with that, I have to learn to deal with my life as it is now. It is not always easy. Actually, it is harder for me to live now than it was 20 years ago. But that is the past, this is my future, and it is only as bright as I am willing to live it. Everything in me says, "Let's keep the battle going." I was born a fighter and I will die fighting.

THIRD CHANCE AT LIFE

☆ ☆ ☆ ☆ ☆

ROLANDE SUMNER

God blessed me with three chances at life. He allowed me to breathe fresh air, eat good food, and live well and safely on three separate occasions… and I took each of those chances for granted.

First Chance

My first chance at life was ordinary. I was raised by a strong single mother. She had high standards and morals and insisted we work hard and take pride in our work. She instilled in us the necessity of treating others with dignity and respect and often said, "You must love someone when they're sick." Compassion was a concept that rang true in my home.

As I grew up, words like advocacy and grassroots were often used. My mom often volunteered with non-profit organizations that focused on women's health, child's education, and the safety of women and families. My grandmother was active in her church and often volunteered to care for the shut-in and foster children in need. My great-grandmother was a pillar in her community. She spent a good deal of her free time motivating and encouraging the youth to pursue their education and live good lives.

So, it was no surprise that I volunteered to join the Army National Guard at 17. My mom could only help one of us with college expenses. Since I was much more of a tomboy and more athletic than my sister, I asked my mom to allow me to sign up. Naturally, she said no. She didn't want her daughter sent to war. I begged and pleaded and made promises to do my chores with a smile and never complain about slimy okra again. After a few months of pleading and a couple of visits from my recruiter, my mom relented. She knew I would swear in on my eighteenth birthday anyway, so she decided to sign my paperwork.

Fast forward seven years as a traditional National Guard and the disaster of 9/11 happened. I felt the call to go to Active Duty. For the following year, I prepared for the AGR (Active Guard Reserve) board. Miraculously, I landed the position on my first try. Over the course of nine years, I volunteered to go on six separate missions, for which I was not selected. In 2011, my command prepared to mobilize, and I was determined to get on that plane.

Again, I found myself pleading my case. At first, I received a no. My command wanted me in the rear to support the elements. I enlisted some help from my immediate leadership. My talents would be best used forward. After some work, I was added to the roster and shipped off a year later.

Halfway into the deployment, my convoy was attacked. My co-driver and I were within seconds of losing our lives. A gunner from another vehicle saved us by finding the assailant and firing back. God blessed me with a second chance at life! I could have easily become one of the 3,249 US Service Members killed in Operation Enduring Freedom (OEF) missions between 2001-2012.

Second Chance

I entered my second chance at life steeped in depression and exhausted. See, up until then I loved my military service but was disappointed in the system. I felt cheated, trapped, and undervalued. I thought that if I went on deployment, I would find a sense of renewed fire for the uniform and return home eager to continue my service. Instead, I felt empty. I felt as if it was all for nothing. I started to regret having survived the attack. I spent the remainder of my deployment isolated and depressed.

When I returned home, I felt worse. I didn't want my family to speak to me or touch me. No one understood what

I was dealing with. How could they? I didn't understand it. Eight months later and a new assignment, I made a decision.

I decided to end it all.

It was a cold February morning as I made my hour and a half long commute to duty. It was a long drill weekend. I packed a bag, preparing to stay the night. I fell asleep while driving on the road and woke up in time to swerve back into my lane of traffic. I lost count of the nights I slept for no more than a two to three-hour cat nap. I lost muscle mass because I wasn't eating right. Some days I barely ate a full meal, other days I ate for two. Then there were the days I didn't eat at all. I was cranky and mean. I fought with my husband and hid from my kids. My work performance suffered. My direct supervisor said I was nothing but drama and blamed me for her decision to quit AGR. Panic attacks were a regular event.

This time when I woke up and drove my car back into the right lane, I made a decision that the next time I fell asleep at the wheel I would allow the car to drive off the bridge and crash. Luckily, God had other plans for me that day. I completed the drive to duty annoyed. I wasn't sleepy any longer, but wide awake. My journey even seemed shorter than usual.

As I walked into the armory, my First Sergeant (1SG) stopped me in the hall and informed me that I would give the MRT class that morning. Yep, you read that correctly. I was the Master Resiliency Trainer (MRT) for the company. I acknowledged his request and shoved my way into my office.

He followed me in and asked if I was ok. I said I was fine. He left, and my annoyance grew stronger. I didn't want to give that stupid class. By that point in my career, I believed Master Resilience Training was a gimmick to convince Soldiers that being shot at was ok. I believed it to be a front to make civilians think the Army cared for us. So, I walked into my direct supervisor's office and asked her to be excused from that detail. I told her what was on my mind and walked back to my office without waiting for a response. A few moments later, she asked me to follow her into our First Sergeant's office. I didn't realize what I had told her or the state of mind I was in, so I thought I was going to get written up because I didn't want to do my duty. Instead, I walked in to the Commander and 1SG waiting on me. The door was closed, and I was asked to take a seat. Then, I was told to hand over my car keys and informed that I would be driven to Moncrief Army Health Clinic.

Third Chance

God loved me so much, He gave me another chance. Let's fast forward...

- ❯ Four psychiatric ward admissions

- ❯ A medical retirement at 19 years and ten and a half months of service

- Moved my family 100 miles to a new city for my great new job

- Experienced my first and only termination from a job two months after being hired

I was depressed and devastated. I felt like a loser. Weeks after I was fired from my first civilian full-time job, I cried and wallowed in my sorrow. Then it hit me like a lightning bolt—I can start my own business.

I had no more excuses. I had all the time in the world. My VA (Veterans Affairs) benefits were good, and my husband was working, so money was ok. We had to live off less, but it was ok. We were happy. I had time to cook for my family and spend more time with my kids at school. I had more time to go to visit the VA and take care of myself. For the first time in my life, I had full autonomy.

Before then, it never dawned on me that God was helping me build my mental and spiritual muscles. It never crossed my mind that my medical retirement and termination from my job was a blessing.

I am now able to glean inspiration and motivation from my story to help other women Veterans on their journey to find themselves. It took me three chances at life to realize that my life was everything I wanted it to be and more. The gift of free will was mine. It was my choice if I wanted to squander this opportunity or live full out and enjoy it. I had a room full of blessings in Heaven waiting for me to bring them to life.

With that realization, I was reborn. I was on fire about life again. I felt like a blooming flower, anxious to share her pollen and spread the energy of joy and abundance.

It took me three chances at life to fully appreciate my blessings. It took me three chances at life to live full out and open my life up to the endless possibilities.

My advice to you is—don't wait. Live now. Do the hard work of adjusting your mindset and learn new ways of seeing the world. Do the hard work necessary to elevate your energy and manifest the life you have always dreamed of.

MY CHALLENGES MADE ME STRONGER

☆ ☆ ☆ ☆ ☆

AKIA CRUTCHFIELD

Change of Plans

Hey, Y'all, hey! I am Akia, but you can call me Kia! I like to think of myself as being a free spirited, spiritual (not religious), and loving person with a lot of that Aries spark! I was not always this person. It has taken much prayer, experience, growth, and meditation to bring me to this position. I am a single mother in the military and it has been trying at times, but it is a struggle I endure with my head held high. I am constantly working on myself and reflecting on how I can improve. I have seen many things in my life and in my military career, but I use my experiences as learning points. I survived military sexual trauma (MST), which further shaped how I handle people in the military and myself. I married young, had a baby, and divorced all before reaching our fourth year of marriage. As I went through my second divorce, I learned very quickly that the male Soldier and female civilian spouse and the female Soldier and male civilian spouse had similar issues when it came to being spurned by the other party and unsupported by the regulations put in place.

Having to prove myself every day as a woman capable of accomplishing the mission was upsetting. I pray that sharing my experiences, whether hardships or amazing, helps every person reading this to understand that the last page is not necessarily the end. It is just a point where you pause, reflect, learn, and then continue to push forward to a better tomorrow.

I joined the Army in 2005 and was not truly prepared for what the universe had in store for me. I was not the Soldier that joined the Army full of grit and desire to serve my country. I always wanted to serve in the military, but I wanted to go to college first. At age 18, I was enrolled in college to major in psychology, held down two jobs, and was saving to move out of my mother's house. Well, of course whatever you plan for is irrelevant, right? Exactly. I was on my way with my plan until one day I was in a car accident that ended up totaling my car. There went my car and my savings to move out.

My mother raised me to be independent and rely on myself, so at that point, I felt like a failure. I decided to quit my jobs, drop out of school, and join the Army. I spoke to a recruiter in November, signed my contract, chose my military occupational specialty (MOS), and shipped out all in December 2005. I was ready to become my own person. Fast forward through training and the Army welcomed me to my first duty station, Fort Myer, Virginia. Now this was the mecca of duty stations. Most people did not know it existed, but those that did knew it was an honor. I knew it and expected everyone affiliated with the legacy to live up to those standards. Boy, was I mistaken. I clearly forgot that people are at the will of their flesh.

The Violation

I was in my unit for all of six months and found myself face to face with a "man" that thought he was going to violate my trust, my body, and my spirit. I was the naive Private, taking work to my room, never taking my foot off the gas. I took some work home that I wanted to get done for an NCO in my company. I spoke to him earlier that day and let him know that he could come by and grab his paperwork from me since my barracks was above the offices. He showed up, I opened the door to give him his paperwork... and I swear it happened so fast.

He pushed me into the room, threw me on the bed, and bit my breast! I could not believe what was happening! I am in the Army, a Soldier, trained and disciplined, at one of the most elite duty stations that has a grand reputation, and now this! I had lived my life with the scars of my past, being taken advantage of, trust broken, body no longer my own but the shared property of others. Now, I had to fight again. But this time I would not let him be another person housed inside of me. Once I realized what was happening, I punched him square in the face and screamed as if my life depended on it, because it did. My life depended on my survival of yet another person thinking that I was not equipped to decide what's right for my body. Once I did that, he looked shocked, as though I had broken some unspoken rule of "how to get taken advantage of 101."

He jumped up and started looking around nervously, signaling for me to stop screaming. At that point, I was furious. I was not screaming for help any longer. I was a lioness, ready to destroy my attacker, ready to give him all the anger I already possessed from previous persons who had thought it was best to hurt me. He ran out, and I just sat there and cried. I cried so hard. I could not believe that the image I had of the Army would become tainted this early in the game. Nevertheless, it had.

Well, the next day I told my leadership what happened. You want to know why? It was not because I wanted justice, it was because I thought I was going to get into trouble for hitting him! Can you believe that? I had been mentally conditioned to believe that protecting my body, my energy, and my spirit could somehow become an issue and cause me to get into trouble. Once I told my leadership what happened, they asked me if I wanted to file a complaint! I asked, "I am not in trouble?" They looked at me crazily and asked, "Why would you be?" I said, "Because I hit him." They quickly answered, "No, you had every right to protect yourself!" I could not believe it. I was 19 years old and finally got confirmation, from an outstanding chain of command, that I could protect my energy from those who wanted to corrupt it!

You Reap What You Sow

I chose not to file a complaint. A year later, he attacked another girl, and then Pandora's box opened. I was called to testify in his court martial. This NCO, with a wife and children, was about to be kicked out of the Army because he lacked self-control. I did not feel bad for him at all. I did, however, feel bad for his wife and children. Then again, I told myself that he should have cared more about his family than I do, so I spoke up. I learned that he had assaulted several females within my unit, and who knows how many more Soldiers he has hurt while serving. I was elated to find out that he would be serving his time and forced to retire early.

Throughout all of that, I remained in love with the Army and continued to be a positive light for others. I went on to marry another Service Member, we were both 19 and lonely. I'll admit, that was not the best decision or situation, but we were in love. Approximately two years into our "marriage," we decided to have a baby and were blessed with a healthy child. For that, I thank God. Then, my suspicion was confirmed. My husband had been cheating on me. He pleaded with me, so I stayed and tried to work it out, not wanting my daughter to struggle with daddy issues as I had. Then we got reassigned to Germany, and poof! He left my daughter and I for another woman. I laugh at it now, but back then I was confused, alone, and sad. I questioned whether I could be in love, happy, and in a committed relationship that I deserved.

About a year later, I met a man who would become my husband five years after our initial meeting. So, at 28 years old and on my second marriage, I thought that time around would be different. I thought it would be better. At least that is what I told myself. I expected something from him that he was unwilling to give me and my daughter. Yes, he was nice to my daughter and I even thought that I should make it work for her sake; but, two years into our marriage, I had a husband at home who did not want to work.

He thought being home was enough because he was not cheating on me like my first husband. He thought being present for our son meant he did not have to make a substantial contribution to our family. He assumed that I would settle. I did not and filed for a divorce. I soon found myself in another fight when he tried to use the system to rake me over the coals and destroy my life. I began to doubt the systems in place even more. I have cried through it all, smiled through it all, prayed through it all, and muscled my way through it all.

Fight the Good Fight

I decided early on to make a change within myself to maintain my sanity. As I continued to fight through life's challenges, I remained resilient. Since being a female leader in the military comes with its own set of challenges, I repeatedly had to prove my worth and my proficiency. I did not allow others to stop me. I continued to grind and claimed my seat at the table ever since I was a Private. I continue to excel. I know many of my female battle buddies who have found it difficult to push through that barrier. I am telling you to keep pushing, do not give up. Stay ahead of the game, stay educated, and remain humble.

I prayed more, meditated, decluttered my home, and became aware of the type of energy I allowed to be in my presence. I even decided to remove toxic people from my life, and I do not feel bad for letting people go any longer. Remember that you have the choice of who you allow to be in your life. Ask yourself this question, "Do I have people or things in my life that build me up spiritually, mentally, and emotionally?" If some of the people in your life do not bring you greatness, you must make the conscious decision to let them go. It will be difficult, but it is well worth it.

Removing toxic people has helped me to focus more on my relationship with God. I will admit, I get lonely at times when I realize that I don't have a team that I can rely on or a confidante that I can trust. But I have come to realize that

God is my everything and I cannot continue to look outside of Him for comfort because I will be disappointed every time.

Given my circumstances, I am blessed to have made it so far in life. I now look at my hardships and challenges as foundational bricks that helped to make me stronger.

FAITHING FEAR-FUL DECISIONS

☆ ☆ ☆ ☆ ☆

NICOLE REDMOND

Wavering Between FEAR and FAITH

There was a point in my life when FEAR ruled my decision-making. I was making FEARful decisions and it led me to walk in the wilderness for a long time, but God is faithful. Today, my decisions are grounded in FAITH—Fully Assured In Trusting Him. There was ONE major decision I made that started this domino effect for me to become the woman that God has molded me into today. But, before I got to this place of acceptance, peace, and active faith, I was faithing FEARful decisions.

FEARful decision #1: I asked a man to marry me out of FEAR because I didn't want to raise a child without a father.

Having the wrong perspective and belief of FEAR can cause grave consequences. The wrong FEAR is false evidence appearing real. Like many women who join the military, our family foundations that we come from can be false evidence appearing real, which impacts how we perceive, judge, think, act, and move.

May 2001

I was waiting for my results from a pregnancy test that I had to take prior to getting a refill on my birth control pills. Certain that my results were negative, I didn't understand what was taking so long for the results to come back. I was stationed at Fort Campbell, Kentucky, and I worked in a supply warehouse in a Main Support Battalion.

I had gone home for lunch that day and noticed that the answering machine was flashing. I pushed the button to listen to the voicemail. It was from the medical clinic stating to return the phone call. At this point I'm thinking, "Why didn't she just leave the results in a voice message?" I called back and spoke with my physician assistant.

"Sergeant Bryant, your pregnancy test came back positive. Congrats, you're going to be a mom."

"Say, what? That can't be right," I responded.

"It is very much accurate, Sergeant Bryant. You are welcome to come and take another pregnancy test. However, I can't prescribe you anymore birth control pills because we now have to enroll you in our pregnancy program."

I was speechless. I got off the phone and my mind zoned out. As I was walking outside, the clouds rolled in and it began to pour down rain. I didn't want to put any child through any mental hardships like I endured growing up.

At that time, I was involved with two men—a high school sweetheart and a man I followed from Germany to Fort Campbell. The latter relationship had been very strained and abusive. He was seven years older than me and previously married. Before we left Germany, he had his first child from another female Soldier he was involved with.

I was 21 years old and the youngest Sergeant in my platoon. I was respected by my fellow Soldiers and senior leadership. I was a hard worker and studied all the necessary regulations about the Army and my job. I loved being a Supply Logistics Specialist—92A! However, when it came to relationships, that was another story.

My relationship experiences began with me losing my virginity at the age of 13, thinking I was pregnant 24 hours afterwards, and becoming excessively promiscuous because I didn't know my worth. Great experience… right? To put the icing on the cake, I joined the Army to get away from home because I absolutely couldn't stand my stepfather. Now, I was pregnant! I eventually told the man I had followed to Campbell that I was pregnant, and he inquired if the baby was his or not. He was manipulating and controlling.

I also told my high school sweetheart that I was pregnant. For some reason, I was hoping he would not want to continue our inconspicuous relationship. However, his response was the total opposite. He didn't care. He wanted me and the baby. He ended up getting out of the military several months later which freed me to break off any communication with him and just focus on my relationship with the man I'd followed. I genuinely wanted to have a fresh start.

Little had changed in our relationship, though. As of matter of fact, it got worst. One day, he found an intimate letter that I had written to my high school sweetheart. He yelled my name which sent chills through my body. Before I knew it, he grabbed my braids and pulled me forcibly toward him. I heard the ripping of my hair from the back of my scalp. He was hollering and smashing the letter in my face. He threw me on the kitchen floor, and I fell hard on my stomach. I was crying and spitting up uncontrollably. I was rushed to the hospital. I told the nurses that I had fallen. They kept me under observation for twenty-four hours. It is only by God's grace and mercy that I didn't lose my baby.

September 2001

On September 11, 2001, we were headed to work when we heard on the radio that a plane had flown into one of the Twin Towers in New York, my birth state. Initially, we didn't pay it any attention because we assumed it was a prank. As it turned out, America was under attack. We both knew that the attacks were going to impact us soon.

February 2002

I was enrolled in Austin Peay State University to attain my associate degree. I was standing outstanding of the college building talking to a good friend. We shared a good laugh, then it felt like a water balloon popped in my pants. I went to the emergency room and the doctors had to induce labor. It was God, me, the nurses, the doctors, and my new baby girl in that room. He was off at a training exercise. She was born at noon on February 12, 2002. She looked like a slim, black Q-tip with a head full of curly black hair.

The idea of getting married started to pop into my head frequently. I proposed to him a couple of months later with sincere ignorance and hope that marriage would redeem me. He accepted my proposal. We had a shotgun wedding on September 9, 2002. Then, we both received orders to go to Korea, with forwarding orders to Fort Hood, Texas.

October 2008

I found illicit pictures of him and another female Soldier at a hotel. There were several pictures of him, her, and his penis. I requested a divorce but told him that if he was willing to go to marriage counseling we could work through it. He declined. So, my decision to see the divorce through came by way of force. It seemed the idea of divorce stressed him to a point of no return. He became very jealous and accused me of seeing another guy (*FEAR*).

After a night out with my girlfriend, I returned home. I called her to let her know I made it safely, then I heard him come in through the garage. I told my girlfriend that I would call her back. I was in the bathroom and before I could finish and get off the toilet, he kicked in the door and put a gun to my head. I started screaming and in that moment my mind flashed images of my daughter without me in her life. He kept the gun on me; he was having a violent mental breakdown.

He expressed bitterly all the mistakes I made prior to the marriage. I managed to get away as he slowly calmed down and started to come back to reality. I ran to my car and drove off in a frantic state. When I got to the highway, I pulled over and began to scream, holler, and fight my steering wheel.

Our divorce was finalized on March 5, 2009, nine days before his thirty-seventh birthday. I was 29 years old then. We will reach the 10-year anniversary of our divorce soon, and I am honored to say that I have forgiven him and most importantly I have forgiven myself.

FAITHing Decisions

I made many mistakes. All of the decisions I made in the earlier part of my life that dealt with SELF were based on false evidence appearing real—*FEAR*. My journey, like many, has been one of trials, tribulations, and struggle. Through it all, God has been ever-present. He has shown me along my journey that the "false evidence" are things in our life setup to confuse, deter, and distract us. I learned that everything I survived was for a purpose.

- **False evidence #1** – Because I grew up in a household where my parents were divorced, I endured and saw a lot of things that appeared real through my natural eyes but were a setup to confuse me about healthy, loving relationships.

- **False evidence #2** – Because I lacked parental nurturing and attention, I sought attention elsewhere, in all the wrong places. I inadvertently used the military as a scapegoat to replace my family.

- **False evidence #3** – Because I understood the idea of a man providing for his family, it became a distraction for avoiding the fact that I lacked the applied wisdom of self-worth. I used poor examples from my adolescent years as a foundation for what I viewed as values. Those misguided values contributed to the ongoing devaluation of my worth as a woman.

> **False evidence #4** – Because I didn't have my father present in my life as I desired and I didn't respect the man my mother married years later, I used that as a deciding factor for asking a man to marry me. I didn't want my child to be without a father. This is what you call false pretense.

"In order to love who you are, you cannot hate the experience that shaped you."

—*Andrea Dykstra*

The difference between FAITHing and FEARful decisions is your belief and perception in HIM and not THEM. HIM is God. THEM are worldly affiliations, which we experience with our eyes and bodies, that change our hearts and minds. This took me many years to accept and apply.

The first step you need to take to start changing how you make decisions is to forgive yourself.

The second step is to challenge every FALSE evidence that has been present in your life.

When you have **Fully Assured In Trusting Him** (God-FAITH), HE will remove all that false evidence and show you the TRUTH about who you are. HE will change your perception to understand that faith is the substance of things hoped for and the evidence of things not seen. It can be a traumatic event to NOT see the evidence of your victory when you are enduring affliction.

Psalm 139:14 (NIV) says, "I praise you because I am *fearfully* and wonderfully made; your works are wonderful, I know that full well." Fearfully made... now I can perceive that! What about you? Don't just stay prayed up, stay FAITHed up!

CHOOSE
YOUR BATTLES

☆ ☆ ☆ ☆ ☆

BRANDY DAVIDSON

In the Beginning...

I joined the military in nineteen hundred and ninety-seven. And I am laughing as I type because if I knew then what I know now, a lot of things would be different. I can't change the past, but I do understand the process was necessary in order to get the understanding that I have now to move forward in life.

Poor me. I was heartbroken, confused about where I was going after high school, and angry because I couldn't control all of the emotions that were taking place within me. I remember sitting in the car and hearing an Army commercial advertising how you can join the Army and go to school for free. It dawned on me that very moment—that is exactly what I will do, join the Army. You can't beat FREE! Mind you, I NEVER wanted to join the military. In fact, when the military recruiters would come to my school, I would just stop by their table for something to write with in class. Who knew that I would succumb to the military?

Fast Forward...

I have always had a smart mouth and an attitude problem, at least that's what everyone said. But I was able to manage it through Basic Training, my first duty station at Fort Lewis, Washington, my second duty station at Camp Casey in Korea, and even my third duty station at Fort Eustis, Virginia. Germany is where all hell broke loose. To this day, I am still thanking God for watching over me and this sword (mouth) of mine.

Yes, I could be the sweetest person you ever met, but cross me and it was a wrap. It didn't matter who you were or what your rank was. Up to that point in my life, I had gone through so much by the age of 22. I never really talked about it much because I couldn't understand it. I held a lot in, which made me more and more angry. I was a ticking timebomb. I had suppressed too much.

Weight

For those of you who didn't know me prior to the military, I was a nice size. A sexy, young thang. But according to military standards, I was overweight. *Really*? I had never been told I was overweight prior to going into the military. Having someone tell me I was overweight played with my psyche. The entire time I was in the military, my weight was up and down. If you failed the weigh-in, you would have to be "taped" (calculations of your body measurements to determine your body fat) to see how much body fat you had on you. If you failed that part, it meant that you failed your weigh-in. Once you were identified as failing the weight part of the Army Physical Fitness Test, you would be counseled and enrolled in a special population program; this meant mandatory Physical Fitness Training (PT) twice a day.

I hated participating in special population PT, especially when I became an NCO (Noncommissioned Officer). Instead of getting in compliance with our weight regulation, I chose to fight back, but not in a positive way. I didn't have a problem passing the PT test, it was just that darn weigh-in that always gave me anxiety. The times I had to get counseled for being overweight were gruesome for whoever had to counsel me. My argument was, "Don't pick and choose who you want to punish for being overweight, just do it straight across the board!" I said it just like that with no tact and no respect for those that outranked me.

Lord, I thank you for keeping your hedge of protection around me.

I can't tell you how many times I disrespected an NCO and never once received an Article 15. Trust me, I am not bragging but letting you know that it was only by God's grace that I can tell the story today.

Where was I? Oh yeah, I was talking about how I put up a fight for being overweight. I remember one occasion when I had to report to my First Sergeant (1SG) to be counseled for being overweight and I boldly told him, "I see too many people, including officers, that look like they are about to pop out their uniform and I don't see anything happening to them!" At that moment, the 1SG told me that he had lost all respect for me and that I needed to get out of his office.

I heard what he said, but it didn't register at that moment. I had a lot of support from my peers, but what was keeping me from losing this weight for good and moving forward with my career? The problem was *me*. I chose to stay angry and not do what needed to be done to keep the weight off and stop the endless cycle. Choosing that route had a major effect on my military career.

My Addiction

While being overweight was my biggest challenge in the military, I also struggled with emotional eating. I didn't think it was a problem back then because I thought I had control over it, but I really didn't. Behind closed doors was a nightmare and it was also where I cried and had my own pity parties. At a tender age, my daughter caught the backlash of my emotions. I was always yelling at her. One minute I was up, the next minute I was down. I was what one would call an emotional mess. I even tried the dating scene and that definitely didn't work either. There was no balance. I focused my attention on being angry with others which allowed me to sink deeper into self-pity.

I know you are probably saying, "Girl, just lose the weight and get on with it!" Yes, it seems easy for you because you had control over something I didn't at the time. In my mind, I didn't want anyone telling me what to do, but I still needed the help.

Why was I so angry? There were numerous reasons why I was angry which kept leading me back through that vicious cycle. The bottom line was that I lacked control. So, I ate! I ate to feel better and to block out the things I had no control over, like my emotions. Controlling my eating or my anger may seem easy to do to you, but it wasn't for me. The more I thought about my chain of command confronting me about my weight, the angrier I would get and the more I would eat.

I had a lot of run-ins with senior enlisted leaders for problems other than just weight. Some things were self-inflicted, and others were legitimate complaints, but I handled them in an immature manner. Again, I am so grateful to God for protecting me from any disciplinary action throughout my career because there were times when it was warranted due to my disrespect of leaders.

My Lessons Learned

I don't regret joining the military. However, I do wish a few things would have gone differently. I later learned that it is not meant for me to fight every battle I face. In other words, pick and choose your battles. I realized this as I grew closer to God and allowed myself to heal. I now understand that every battle is not meant to be fought by me. Do yourself a favor and learn the difference. I fought a lot of battles that I should not have. My goal now is to share the lessons I learned from that with anyone who will listen. I do not want anyone to repeat the mistakes I made.

Early in my life and during my career, I needed anger management classes along with counseling because I was broken and never took the time to restore myself. At that time, I didn't know I needed healing. I would put on a mask every day before walking out of my house for work. I didn't receive any help because I was afraid to admit that I really had some problems and that I needed help to get through them. My career in the military could have taken a turn for the better, who knows.

My last piece of advice to those personnel serving, especially leaders, is a reminder that no one is perfect. If you feel that you are spiraling out of control, seek help. It is hard to lead others when you keep going in circles yourself. It was for me. Getting help does not mean that you are weak or incompetent; it is a sign of strength.

STEPPING OUT OF RAGE AND INTO JOY

☆ ☆ ☆ ☆ ☆

TERESA JOY EDLOE

"Don't be dejected and sad, for the joy of the
Lord is your strength!"

—*Nehemiah 8:10 (NLT)*

Joining the US Air Force (USAF) taught me so much about life, how to be of service, and how to persevere. The USAF showed me how important and rewarding it was to serve a mission bigger than myself. I am thankful and continuously humbled by that beautiful lesson. Yet, I found myself still seeking. I wanted to join a mission in the USAF where I could feel a deeper purpose. I had the honor of being a part of a unique opportunity to be both an Active Duty military member and a federal agent for the USAF. When I entered that career field, I was excited but naïve and did not understand the depth of criminality nor the depth of hidden pain buried deep in my mind.

Bad Guys Look Just Like Good Guys

As a federal investigator in a fast-paced career field, I was introduced to investigating all types of crimes. My focus was on sexually related crimes to include child molestation and rape. I had no idea the frequency of these crimes. We had more cases than we could keep up with. I was in shock. It felt like there were more bad guys than good guys, and I felt so overwhelmed. I didn't know anything about the sickness of child pornography until I worked in that field. I had to attempt to compartmentalize what I saw because trying to understand or analyze how someone could do such things was intolerable. Over time, I internally became more and more unable to tolerate the environment I had exposed myself to; yet, I still felt a strong drive to help those that didn't have a voice. However, here I was struggling to find my own voice to say I need help. I pressed forward and became a child forensic interviewer. I was humbled and honored to do my best to create a safe place for a child to disclose the abuse they experienced. I remember every child I interviewed and connected with during that process, but after the interviews I never processed the experience. I didn't allow myself to cry or become angry about the fact that someone could do that to a child. I didn't know how or that it was ok to feel heartbreak for those children. It wasn't part of my training or tools.

I spent long days working into the night and going home to self-medicate so that I could sleep, only to wake up from a dream about work, then get up and do it all over again. I wondered if anyone else was having problems, or was I being weak and too sensitive? Everyone else seemed pretty tough, they didn't complain, and they worked hard. The more I talked about violations, the more irritated, intolerant, and angry I felt. On the outside I remained poised and professional, but on the inside rage was brewing.

Combat Zone, Here I Come

I volunteered to deploy to a combat zone in the Middle East. The first time my building shook and my window rattled, I knew I was not in Kansas anymore. I remember being on the phone with a loved one while we got attacked. I calmly made up a lie to get off the phone, but on the inside my whole nervous system was shook. I looked around and no one was having an honest conversation about being afraid or anxious. I was dealing with some serious anxiety. Within a short period of time after returning from Iraq, I spoke to a therapist. I told her it felt like I was having a heart attack, like my heart was going to come right out. She said, "Sounds like you have anxiety." I didn't really understand anxiety, but I wanted to know what I needed to do because I had to get back to work. I stepped out of my office for 30 minutes to talk to her, like we could fix this really quick and then I could get back to work. Not doing my job was not an option. The anxiety was so bad it felt like I was trembling like a washing machine and people could see it. Maybe they could.

The Unraveling: Anger

The strong desire to "Protect and Serve" others had a direct correlation to my own past that I was not consciously aware of. I was a workaholic, and when I wasn't working, I spent time volunteering and working out at a local mixed martial arts gym. I was a "punching bag," getting my butt kicked by men who were professional fighters. It was how I unconsciously dealt with my pain, anger, and stress from the compounding emotional trauma I was not aware of. I realize now that I was addicted to physical pain; it distracted me from the deep emotional trauma I experienced. I equated this to the girls I knew growing up that were cutters. They cut their bodies to release deep emotional pain that built up like a pressure cooker. I knew stress from the job was normal, but I had no idea how deeply it was affecting me nor why.

Once I was out of the military and no longer doing law enforcement, I was at a loss. I barely left my apartment due to dealing with severe depression, constant ruminations, and anger. Vodka was my best friend. Along with my emotional stress, I was now dealing with chronic pain from physical inflammations derived from nerve damage and arthritis. I used to be a fitness instructor and now I was very inactive. I had developed bad posture, gained weight, and at times I could not get out of bed for long periods of time. I didn't realize this is what my anger looked like. I was holding within my body the energy of my trauma and my rage, and I hurt daily. In addition, I was embarrassed by my lack of emotional control, so I isolated myself from people. Suicidal ideations crept into my mind, but I would lie about it, even to my therapist.

Everything irritated me. And if someone joked about violating someone, I felt enraged. I was afraid of my rage, afraid of losing control, and I didn't know how to deal with it. I tried my best to hide it, but it felt intense, explosive, and violent. I was so good at putting on a brave face that when I really needed support even people that knew me for a long time didn't know it. I was told how blessed I was, but I just couldn't find the JOY in my situation. I was stuck.

With God I Found My Joy

Volunteer work, getting back into martial arts, being in nature, and dancing helped me to stay connected to God. Those things are my therapy and the best medicine. Serving the community as the Air Force taught me, "service before self," was actually instrumental in my own healing, allowing me to connect with people and God and come out of isolation. When I start to feel confused or anxious, the first thing I do now is not call people, I pray. I feel so much gratitude that most of my prayer is just giving thanks.

I can't stress enough the importance of mental health services for military and law enforcement and frankly for anyone who needs it. When I was in the military, going over to the mental health unit had a bad stigma, but I encourage you to do it. It takes strength and bravery to ask for help. It's a great gift of self-love. We are humans with hearts, and sometimes we hurt for the people we try to help. At other times, we just hurt. Sometimes we do jobs that expose us to environments which are not the norm. We need to be able to talk about it, get mad, cry, or feel upset. It is so important to understand that when we don't feel well, we can't be of service to others.

We are taught to put on a brave face, but that is not the answer because it does not work. I kept doing that until I could no longer do the mission. I've thought to myself that if I had got on my knees more and prayed, maybe I would still be able to do my job. If I had sought mental health treatment much earlier, maybe I'd still be in the military. I smiled and laughed with my colleagues, but inside I felt I had failed. I couldn't help anyone. I was weak. Those were the lies I told myself. The truth is I did the best I could, so now I walk with my head held high. Whether an experience lasts for a moment or a season, there is always a reason. I served my purpose.

I used to depend on people for answers, so looking to God was actually a new concept for me. Learning to trust in God and trust in myself was what I needed. Another great and important tool was understanding that healing takes time. It takes as long as it takes. Love yourself and be patient. And as the feelings come up, let them come. When guilt, shame, or other painful feelings show up, I say, "I acknowledge you, but you are not in charge today. Thank you for showing up and providing me with an opportunity to heal."

I encourage you to stay connected to God, your Source, your Higher Power who is within you and around you. Find what works for you. I use chanting meditation, positive affirmations, and being in nature—the sun is rejuvenating, energizing, and healing. My experiences have taught me that I must stay connected to God in everything I do. I realize now that self-love is a lifelong, consistent, and repetitive practice. It is not selfish to take care of yourself first. Self-love is required in order to succeed. It is our intention and knowing who we ultimately serve that gets us through the tough times. Spend intimate time with God. Think about how you can be of service to others and you will continue to honor God and yourself!

"The Lord is my strength and shield. I trust him with all my heart. He helps me, and my heart is filled with joy."— Psalm 28:7 (NLT)

THE PRICE OF MY NO

☆ ☆ ☆ ☆ ☆

ELLA SMART

Yes to Everything

I was the girl who sat at the back of the classroom, shy and timid. I never believed in myself. I was so self-conscious, afraid, non-confrontational, and a typical people pleaser with very low self-esteem. My nature then was passive-aggressive and totally nonassertive. So, you can imagine how proud of myself I was at a recent small group meeting, with about ninety five percent of us as single moms supporting one another. To listen to myself and to see the excitement on the faces of the ladies as I gave them some very critical advice and answers from my experience was a huge 'aha' moment for me.

It feels humbling but great to finally embrace the fact that I have come a long way and that I am thriving gracefully. The courage to be transparent and vulnerable about my journey, and to see my story still unfolding but helping another woman is such an encouragement to me.

I was a "yes to everything" kind of girl!

There was a time when I had no major plans for my life. I typically went anywhere with the flow of things and people. I didn't know me, and I wasn't even trying to find me. I was contained and content where I was. I let my passive-aggressive nature open the door for people to dictate life to me. I was the definition of any and everyone's pushover. I guess you can agree with me here in one of my quotes crafted from my experience: *A woman who does not know her self-worth will trade her values for a boundary-less life.* She is like a city without walls, vulnerable to attacks and open to anything passing by. I didn't know me. I wasn't looking for me. So, there was nothing about me to value enough for me to set boundaries for myself. I was too afraid to hurt anyone at the expense of how I felt or how they made me feel. I was a yes to everything girl.

Lost in a Living Hell

While I was not a promiscuous woman, my kind of stupidity and foolishness then is what I call a learned behavior. A product born from my background. I was badly labeled and always called negative names, which affected my self-esteem. I grew up a follower, chasing after people's love and affirmation. So, I would do everything to be loved and accepted or just to fit in. My subtle form of manipulation was spiced with many fake performances.

I was broken in a weird way! Just like a bottomless pit with an insatiable appetite, the deep void in me was never satisfied. I could never fit in! Yet, I wasn't even looking for the lost me. My late pastor, Paul Irabor, would always say to me, "There is a reason why you don't fit in!"

It was at this broken and unhealthy stage of my life that I married my Soldier. I was hungrily looking for love, security, and significance in all the wrong places. Worse still, I went into my marriage expecting him to meet those needs. He was a broken man and my brokenness attracted him to me. We became two broken people who could not raise whole children.

We were both wounded by life and walking on broken bones while the pain of our brokenness fed on the open fertile soil of the military life. It was a place where he had full access and friends who were connected to him for the same dysfunction. He drank heavily to numb his pain and feed his disease. His behavior was mostly altered by alcohol and the multiple women in his life. He became very aggressive and abusive. My heart was his doormat! He would abuse me verbally, mentally, and physically. I was isolated from the military wives and never participated in activities with other families. Many times, he abandoned me and our little children for days and months. I became a full wide-eyed spectator of my own life. I knew marriage was supposed to be better than what I had long tolerated.

The silent, distant whispers from the lost me within would always remind me that I deserved more and better. But I was too afraid to demand more. I settled in my comfort because the fear of change was too scary and unfamiliar. The unrealistic expectation I came into marriage with gave birth to a deep premeditated resentment for him. I contemplated suicide as my life was a living hell. I gave up everything and gave myself away hoping to be chosen, only to end up being rejected over and over again in torture and many heartbreaks.

Finding the Lost Me

I learned the truth the hard way. I realized that my life was layered with many toxic patterns. I faced the same experience of betrayal, rejection, and abandonment from different people at different times. I lived like a victim and stayed powerless and helpless. Yet, my marriage and the military life were the fires that brought all of my broken pieces to the surface. I had to decide whether to pick up the pieces or pretend they didn't exist.

To beat the giant called Old Ella and interrupt her pattern, I had to confront my fears by unveiling layers of lies I had lived in and allowed to shape my identity for years. I had to teach myself that I'm worth more than not being chosen or accepted by people who are just as broken and wounded as me.

I lost a piece of my true self every time I said yes to the lies that promised love and acceptance. I had to find me by learning to say no in order to say yes to who I am meant to be. Today, I've learned to reclaim my "no" and the many wasted years. What I can't take back is a lesson turned into a weapon of growth. My courage to finally say no to abuse, domestic violence, adultery, and a toxic marriage has left me divorced and alone, but not lonely. The new me understands the difference now.

My "no" came with a price that I am still paying. One that may take years to pay. Although I have found me, I am still evolving. The real me was always there but hidden behind lies. I have learned that I'm beautiful, powerful, and strong. God has a plan for me! I know this to be true and found encouragement in 1 Corinthians 13:11, which states, "When I was a child, I spoke and thought and reasoned as a child. But when I grew up, I put away childish things" NLT. I interpret this Scripture to mean, "When I was a child, I did not know me, and I had no choices. Now that I am an adult, I no longer settle in excuses by taking refuge in lies. I get to choose my experiences and take ownership for my choices." I know that God is a restorer. He is able to weave our past mistakes into His original plan for us, and that's the hope of my "no."

It took a lot of courage to finally reclaim my no after many years of settling into a false yes instead of a no from a healthy place. There were things I had to unlearn in order to learn and set healthy boundaries in place as I prepare for my best yes that God ordained for me before the foundations of the world. How I steward this season is key to my next season, both for me and my children. I am raising four precious children alone, but this time I am whole and complete in Christ. I am no longer looking to people for my significance. I am finally reclaiming my no and giving God my best yes.

A COMBAT FEMALE VETERAN AND LIFE AFTER WAR

☆ ☆ ☆ ☆ ☆

SANDRA G. ROBINSON

"Have I not commanded you? Be strong and of good courage; do not be afraid, nor be dismayed, for the Lord your God is with you wherever you go."

—*Joshua 1:9 (NKJV)*

A Wake-Up Call

In November of 1990, while a junior in nursing school, my life took a very serious and surprising turn. I received a call one morning at about 4:00 a.m. informing me that my unit would be mobilizing in support of Operation Desert Shield. I was going to war.

I had been hearing about Operation Desert Shield in the news. But, despite being in the Army Reserves and despite our nation's interests overseas, I never expected to be going to war. Suddenly I was no longer a Reservist but on Active Duty. That brief call, received in the middle of the night, was a wake-up call. At the time, I felt like life as I knew it was ending. Reality continued to set in as we prepared to deploy.

Anxieties were high on many fronts. There was, of course, the natural fear of war itself. And, what would life be like when I came back home? Operation Desert Storm was really the first known conflict since the Vietnam War, and we all know how the Veterans of *that* war were treated upon their return, if they even made it back. There was also the matter of my personal life and having to say goodbye to my college sweetheart. That was so very hard for both of us. Just before I left, he surprised me by proposing. I told him we would get married upon my return. That was a promise made and something I looked forward to.

Deployment

On January 17, 1991, my unit left for Saudi Arabia, landing in an active war zone. The war, Operation Desert Storm, officially started that very day. I volunteered to serve my country and knew the risks but *knowing* something and *living it* are two different things. I couldn't believe it was actually happening. We were at war. My unit (comprised of hundreds of men and twelve young females) had completed Basic Training, as well as Advanced Individual Training (AIT) a few years prior, but we weren't adequately prepared for war. *I wasn't prepared for war.* But there I was standing in the sand with a 50-pound rucksack on my back and an M16 in my hand.

Desert Fever

As a Transportation Unit, we didn't stay together. We were separated into teams and attached to other units, acting as support. We traveled about eight hours behind the ground Troops, tasked with making sure they received food, water, ammo, and medical supplies. The twelve women were spread among the smaller teams and weren't allowed to ride together. Sometimes, I would go weeks without even seeing another female.

We slept in the same tents as our male peers when in camp. When traveling, which was most of the time, we slept upright in our trucks or on the hoods of our vehicles. There were no trees, no bushes, no privacy, nothing but sand. It was rough, especially the lack of privacy. But it got even worse. Somehow, the military had forgotten about us females and our menstrual cycles! There were no feminine supplies, and we were left on our own to improvise until the problem was remedied. Water, another scarce commodity, was closely rationed each day.

Our conditions further deteriorated once we entered Iraq—enemy territory. There we had limited food, water, supplies… and we went 30 days without ever changing our clothes!

Lost… or Forgotten?

"Jesus said to him, 'Have I been with you so long, and yet you have not known Me, Philip? He who has seen Me has seen the Father; so how can you say, 'Show us the Father'?"

—*John 14:9 (NKJV)*

Our team was in constant fear of being attacked; we were skirting scud missiles and navigating around decapitated bodies. My biggest concern through all of that wasn't that I was going to get killed, nor was it being stared at, groped, or even raped by male Soldiers. My greatest concern was that I would be forgotten back home. After all, we received so few letters. I was worried that I would end up being away for so long that no one would remember me, not even my fiancé. I was afraid that in addition to the conveniences of the civilian world and the feeling of safety I'd lost in service to my country, he'd stop loving me. That fear weighed heavily on my heart, and I spent a lot of time in prayer over it.

Going Home

I was thankful when the war ended. I was eager to travel back to the United States. But, with the end of our tour, new concerns took hold. We began to hear stories about people who were angry about the war and were taking it out on Soldiers. Those stories were fragmented and confusing, leaving too much room for speculation. (Remember that the communication infrastructure wasn't built up like it is today.)

But alas, we were going home.

When our plane touched down in Virginia, I was nervous. I was so worried about what I was going to find. But no amount of preparation could have prepared me for the welcome I received when I got off that plane. My family and my fiancé were there waiting for me! They hadn't forgotten about me after all! The experience was almost overwhelming.

Life After War

"Precious in the sight of the Lord is the death of his saints."

—Psalm 116:15 (ESV)

I returned to college. It wasn't easy, but my belief and faith carried me through. In 1992, I earned a bachelor of science degree in nursing. In 1993, I married by fiancé. In August 1995, I gave birth to my son, David. Then, in September 1995, my husband was killed in a tragic car accident.

War was hard. Losing my husband was much harder. He had waited for me when I went off to war. And now, he was gone.

Anyone who has suffered a loss of this magnitude knows how difficult it is to tell the story of your grief. The pain was overwhelming. The visions in my mind's eye mingled—visions of the decapitated bodies I'd seen in Iraq and the image of my husband's body. It was too much, and I found myself at a crossroads. I had to decide whether to live or to die. That decision took me many months to make, as I wallowed in severe depression.

In the end, my Christian values wouldn't allow me to take my own life. God told me that my husband was His, as am I.

> "For if we live, we live to the Lord; and if we die,
> we die to the Lord. Therefore, whether we live or die,
> we are the Lord's."
>
> —*Romans 14:8 (NKJV)*

Re-Awakening

I willed myself to rise. I was a warrior, a fighter, a survivor.

It was God who wiped the tears from my eyes. I was His child, and He had promised to never leave me. It was I who had forgotten to ask God for help. Instead, I'd let sorrow get the best of me. I asked God to fix me, and He did. He filled the empty spaces and reminded me that my life was not over. He wasn't done with me yet.

I woke up one morning soon after and decided to buy a house, start a business, return to nursing, and reinvent myself. Then, in the year 2000, I met my knight in shining armor, my husband, Bruce Wilson. God kept His promise to care for me.

Conclusion

After riding the rollercoaster of life, I feel certain that nobody ever really knows what's coming, nor can they control it. Take me for example. I thought I had life all planned out before my deployment, then life went and sprung something entirely different on me, forever changing my course. But, through my military service, my loss, and my consequent struggles, I learned an invaluable lesson. You can fight your new reality, as I did when disaster struck my life, or you can accept that your world has changed and *choose* to move toward recovery.

With God's help, I began to release my need for control and thus began to truly heal. Since childhood I've lived by the adage, "If I do my best, God will do the rest." That has proven to be true over and over again. When I went to Him in prayer, while putting my best foot forward, He fixed it. In my grief, however, I'd forgotten.

Today, I continue to ask God daily to direct my plans so that I can go out and do the work He would have me do. My hope for you, as you read my story, is that you identify with my trials in some way and learn to make the best of *your life after war*.

Please don't give up. Good luck and Godspeed.

STRENGTH
TO SERVE

WHEN SELF IS LOST

☆ ☆ ☆ ☆ ☆

ERICA WILKERSON

A Sign

You've been waiting and waiting to get your orders. So, you go into work early to check your mail and there it is—the email from your branch manager. There is a pause, the breath is held, and the open button is hit. Yes, finally a request for orders (RFO) is there. I was going back close to home. This was the beginning of my journey back to self. I just did not know it yet.

I had been a Captain for about three years at that point, so I was ready to go to a new duty station to get some leadership experience as possibly a clinical nurse manager. By that time, I had also had plenty of experience as a floor nurse in labor and delivery. Although I knew I would be going to a bigger facility, I was ready and willing to take on that challenge. I had great mentors and friends that had guided me when I filled the role of the clinical nurse manager in their absence. My family was also glad for us to come closer to our hometown since we had been away for a couple of years and we had a new daughter they really had not had a chance to interact with on a regular basis. The hard part as always when you leave a duty station is the people. That was the hardest part and the most difficult duty station I had to leave because of the wonderful friends I made.

I knew I needed to move in order to continue to grow in my career. You will face difficult decisions every day that need to be made. Make them with certainty, especially if they are fulfilling a need for you while complementing the mission of the military. Although the mission is first, you and your well-being also have to be priority. If the Soldier is not functioning at 100 percent, then the mission is at risk anyway.

Here I was going through the motions of a move—excited, sad, anxious, a whole range of the what-ifs, and stressing. I had my paperwork together for the move and a date ready for them to pick up our household goods. The day arrived that you get all your stuff packed up and ready to go. An hour went by, no one showed. No big deal, they always give you a window. Well, I looked up and it was lunch time and I still had not heard anything from the moving company. I had done multiple moves by that time that had worked like clockwork, so this was starting not to feel right. Hmm. I was getting a little impatient, so I decided to give the office a call to check the status.

When I tell you I almost lost my rank and religion that day, because all I heard was, "We do not have you on the schedule." I can still feel my stomach turning in knots and my chest tightening with shear rage and emotion. I know my blood pressure was sky high. I could not even think, and I barely remember driving to the household goods office after slamming the phone down. Nobody but the Lord got me together by the time I walked into that office. Two days later, a moving company came. They stayed at my house packing until midnight. Yes, you read correctly, midnight. I knew this was a bad sign of things to come.

Another Sign

There was a bright spot in all the mess. We found out we were pregnant during that transition. That helped to explain some of the craziness I was feeling inside. We were excited, especially since we knew we would be closer to family. They would be able to be there basically from the beginning. Even though this was great news, it added another layer of emotions to an already high stress time. My family and I were in transition, my medical records were in transition, my furniture was in transition, and we were traveling with kids and a golden retriever. Oh yeah, I forgot to mention that my cat I had for eight years suddenly went missing a week before we moved out. I had to take a confirmed pregnancy test at a random military base so that it would be in the military system. Not to mention we were somewhat homeless, sometimes staying at hotels or with family. Oh the joys of moving!

On one of my last days at my old duty station, I was leaving the hospital and I noticed a crow as I walked down the sidewalk. As I got closer to him, he flew towards me. I yelled at the crow and said "Stop!" He flew back up to the branch he had been sitting on. But as soon as I started walking again, he came towards me again. I do not know what made me say to him, "I know," but he understood and flew away. We were headed out to the new duty station, so I never brought up that story to anyone.

Tricare was able to get an ultrasound scheduled for me at one of the local hospitals since I was still in-processing. We were all excited; the whole family went with us for the ultrasound. I was the only one that could go back into the exam room. The technician moved the cursor around and around, clicking and clacking on the machine. I could tell she was going through her normal routine. Suddenly, the clicking and clacking slowed down. She looked up a couple of times. I could see the uneasiness come over her, so I started to get uneasy as well. I put two and two together because I am a labor and delivery nurse. So, I just asked her, "Can you not find the heartbeat?" Her long pause told me everything I needed to know. She finally said, "I have to have the radiologist come in, I'm not all..." I cut her off and told her that I was a labor and delivery nurse, then she confirmed it.

The rest was kind of a blur. I remember going to the bathroom crying and getting myself together enough to face my family. My husband asked, "How did everything go? Did they give you pictures?" I lost it emotionally right in the parking lot and almost fell to the ground. He had to catch me. I blurted out, "They said the baby doesn't have a heartbeat!"

What I didn't say about the crow encounter was that somehow I felt he was trying to tell me that something was wrong with my baby. In some mythology, crows are a sign for death.

Listen to the Signs

Even though my world was totally rocked, I had to get up, continue in-processing, figure out what my next steps would be, and prepare for surgery. Life has a way of getting your attention when you keep ignoring the signs given, and that loss taught me to pay better attention to myself and to take time out for self-care. The truth is, I was taking care of everyone but myself. I had not been feeling like myself for a while, which was another reason why I thought the move would be good. My body was physically, mentally, and emotionally worn out. As Soldiers, we are taught to just suck it up, but everyone has a breaking point.

My child was gone and now I was at a unit with strangers, feeling as if I would have to explain my sudden absence to everyone. Then, a crazy thing happened. The doctor asked me, the patient, "How much time do you need?" I must have given him the craziest look because he started talking about the recovery time, not just physically but mentally.

Self-care is now a key foundation in my life. I did not know it then, but that doctor was laying the foundation for me to recognize what I needed. I had to find out where Erica had gone. Yes, my loss was terrible and will always stay with me, but the me now will never put my well-being in jeopardy again; my loss will serve as a reminder.

I eventually went back to work and integrated just fine as a floor nurse for about six months. Then the time came and I was chosen to be clinical nurse manager of one of the units. The Lord will always pull you through. I share my story to remind you that yes, you are going to face adversities, but you will also make it through. Life gets hectic, but I want you to remember that if your total well-being is not good, then you truly are not helping anyone else. You are not able to give your all to work, family, friends, and most of all, yourself. The airlines even tell you to put your oxygen mask on before you help anyone else.

Find a method or two, or three, of self-care routines that work for you and do them on a regular basis. Your method could be journaling to release your thoughts, a weekly phone call to check in with someone, practicing mindfulness throughout the day, meditating, yoga, daily affirmations, or unplugging from everything for an hour each day. Just try something to keep you grounded. There is something for everyone.

Make this a priority. Ask friends and family, or a mentor or coach to keep you accountable. Reach out for professional help or join a support group if you have experienced loss. I decided to end my career by retiring and that this move would be my last one connected to the Army. I listened to that internal voice this time. I want you to have the best life you can have and not ignore life's signs. When those signs pop up, institute tools that will help you early in the process. You can have it all, as long as you have and maintain a strong foundation of self.

IS THIS IT?

☆ ☆ ☆ ☆ ☆

THERESA ALEXIS

This Is Us

"How long are you going to carry this with you, Lucas?!"

Those words pierced through my entire soul as they were shouted at me by a Staff Sergeant who was due to deploy with me in the early fall of 2008. He couldn't comprehend or relate to what I was feeling inside. He wasn't in my shoes. How could someone be so heartless to think that I'd get over a very traumatic situation so easily? It had only been a few months since *it* happened, and I was going to need a lot more time than a measly few months to heal both internally and externally.

In the fall of 2006, right after I graduated from high school, I enlisted in the United States Marine Corps. I can still smell the sweat, fear, and anxiety from all the people who surrounded me in the van that took us to Parris Island, South Carolina. It all started with those yellow footprints.

From boot camp, Marine Combat Training (MCT), military occupational specialty (MOS) school, and finally to the fleet, life seemed to be hopeful and full of adventure. I met a lot of new and seasoned Marines from all walks of life and from a variety of states and countries. This gave me a fresh outlook and new perspective when it came to people and seasons in life. Diversity was one of the greatest things I was exposed to during my military career.

Then, there was this guy. He was tall, stocky, had creamed coffee colored skin, a fresh smile, and a patch of light brown specks (freckles) on his face. I remember it like it was yesterday; he noticed me before I noticed him. He made every effort to be in my presence and unbeknown to me, he had a *thing* for me. We were stationed at Camp Lejeune, North Carolina, at the time and both somewhat new to the fleet. Months passed and as we spent time together, we got closer and our feelings for each other deepened. Eleven months after meeting, Robert and I married. I'll be honest, I didn't plan to be married while serving and I wasn't truly prepared for what lie ahead for us as a dual Active Duty couple. Nevertheless, we loved each other, and we had the potential to grow spiritually and professionally with each other and build a legacy together. Not to mention, I was thrilled to take on his last name, Lucas.

Just two months after matrimony, Robert and I found out we were pregnant. While we were surprised by how quickly it happened, we were overjoyed at the possibility of being parents and sharing our life with another human being. Children are a unique gift and a reflection of a love that has evolved. We were both scheduled to deploy, but obviously I would stay in garrison now due to the pregnancy. Weeks and months went by and Robert went off to Mojave Viper in Twentynine Palms, California, to train for his upcoming deployment.

I was nervous, yet I knew the call and the sacrifice we both signed up for. I was positive about everything, but deep down inside, I was sort of terrified. I'd never been married, never been pregnant, and never had to kiss my husband goodbye to go train for a deployment. It was all new and foreign to me and I had to lean on seasoned dual-military couples to help me through that type of transition. Faith was the best thing Robert and I incorporated into our lifestyle when we got married, and it grew stronger as we went through things in the military and within our marriage.

This Can't Be

Then all of a sudden, *it* happened. What is *it*? *It* is the thing that people don't think about or know how to handle unless they go through it, read about it, or study it. *It* is that unspoken thing that is so loud and so obvious that you cannot deny it exists. *It* for me was waking up to excruciating cramps and bleeding while my husband was over two thousand miles away. This couldn't be! I panicked and jumped up off the couch that I was sleeping on. I woke up my friend, whose house I stayed the night over, and she rushed me to Camp Lejeune Naval Hospital Emergency Room. We waited and waited and waited some more. Minutes seemed like hours as I prayed that what was happening to me was not what I suspected. The uncertainty I felt sitting in the waiting room with my friend began to devour me and I almost couldn't catch my breath. My husband was still far away and unaware. And although my friend sat next to me, I felt so alone.

Finally, the doctor called us back and gave me a full exam to figure out why I was having pain and bleeding. Around that time, I was twenty weeks pregnant, the halfway point, and the doctor couldn't find the heartbeat. The beat that symbolizes the existence of life. The beat that distinguishes a living soul from that of inorganic matter. The beat that made my heart sing praises to the God I serve and the beat that I knew *had* to be there, although I couldn't see it. My mind was clouded and overwhelmed by fear and anxiety as the doctor kept talking. He finally turned the screen in my direction and showed me the twin sacks that looked strange and showed no heartbeats.

Twins? What? When? How?

Now I had even more emotions flooding through me. I didn't even know I was carrying twins. The doctor gave a bunch of confusing explanations, one being that maybe I was only ten weeks instead of twenty weeks. Afterwards, he discharged me and gave me orders to go home and "wait it out." My friend who accompanied me to the Naval Hospital immediately took me to the Emergency Room at Onslow Memorial Hospital and that was where I actually delivered the babies. That day seemed long and mentally excruciating. A Red Cross message was finally sent out to my husband. His mother, who was the closest relative to us at the time, drove up to relieve my friend and be by my side. I couldn't look at her, talk to her, or acknowledge her presence for fear that my emotions would burst and I'd just be a complete crying mess.

How could this happen to me? What did I do to deserve this?

Those were the thoughts that raced through my mind and caused me to fall into a deep depressive state. I felt guilty, as if God was punishing me for something I had done in the past. My husband was able to come home for one week while I was on bedrest. He had to leave as I was checking out for my second week of convalescent leave. I knew he had to go, but with everything that had just happened it was hard for me to fathom. I couldn't eat, sleep, or function properly. And while all this went on, I kept it to myself.

Fight Through This

Returning to work was very difficult because there was a flood of questions when I returned in regular desert cammies and not the pregnant uniform. When I couldn't be at work without crying or staring off into the distance constantly, I went to my Officer in Charge (OIC) and told him what I was experiencing. The Staff Noncommissioned Officer who was in my chain of command was out on vacation, so I had no choice but to go to this OIC and ask for help. Instead of providing me with the assistance I needed, he immediately put me on the roster to deploy. As if I needed another battle to fight, I had to jump through hoops in this new Command to not only get help, but to not look like a dirtbag who was just trying to get out of a deployment.

For as long as I can remember, I've had to fight. I had to fight constantly throughout my childhood, fight to get away from my childhood trauma, and now I was fighting to get the proper care I needed within the military for something that wasn't even my fault. I finally sought out mental health care at the Naval Hospital and was put on meds for depression, anxiety, and insomnia. I also went to counseling for the loss of my babies and it helped me tremendously in the healing process. It took months, that turned into years, for me to feel somewhat like myself again and acknowledge that God was not at fault in my babies passing. He had never left my side when I was going through that traumatic experience. The biggest contributions to my healing during that time were my faith in God and the support I received from people of faith who gave me space and time when I needed it.

I never imagined I would go through something like that in my life. Nevertheless, I truly believe that everything happens for a reason and no experience, whether good or bad, is wasted. I have been able to share my testimonies, instill hope, and empower and inspire women across the globe. My transparency has allowed other women to break free from mental bondage and resulted in me stepping out and stepping up to be the woman I was called to be, not just for myself but for those around me. As military women we have to fight a lot harder to prove ourselves, rise above our adversities, and change the way the world perceives us. Acknowledging that you need help or that you're not completely ok is not a sign of weakness. It takes intestinal fortitude to be able to acknowledge a flaw, shortcoming, or issue. When we do, we can get the help we need and we will be able to help someone else who may have a similar issue.

THE SAVING GRACE OF STORYTELLING WITH SHAKESPEARE

☆ ☆ ☆ ☆ ☆

ROBIN LUDWIG

Destined to Serve

I was born on Sheppard Air Force Base during the Reagan era. My favorite childhood playgrounds included F-16 cockpits and airplane hangars that echoed with the sound of combat boots. To this day, I can't help but smile when I encounter that intoxicating mixture of grease, old rubber, resin, and jet fuel. I was raised on *MASH* reruns, *TOPGUN*, and *Tour of Duty*. After my father's retirement from the Air Force, I became known as a preacher's kid, but I prided myself on first being a military brat.

Based on my upbringing, it should have come as no surprise when I decided to join the Air National Guard halfway through college. I went on to become a high school English teacher, proudly serving my country along the way. The Air Force always felt like my extended family. The filial love I bore for my brothers and sisters-in-arms led me to overlook a multitude of injustices during the first half of my military career. Somewhere along the way, the consistent drip of misogynistic comments and sexist attitudes began to wear on my soul. It took nearly fifteen years to bury my innate optimism under mounds of cynicism. There was a strange comfort in knowing I wasn't alone; countless military women walked that same road of degradation.

As a young Airman, I learned there was an unspoken, unwritten manual for female behavior in the military. I accidentally learned this while eating a banana at my workstation. My Commander happened to grace my presence and haunt my thoughts with an unforgettable comment, "Oh Airman! Don't do that to this old man, my heart can't take it!" He stood there, staring as I took a bite. It took everything within my power to choke down my natural disgusted response. The military bearing that had been so deeply ingrained in me during Basic Training kept my disdain vaulted behind sealed lips. The proper response from a young Airman to a full bird Colonel? Stand in respect and smile politely. I became well-versed in this subservient and ingratiating behavior in order to survive among the ranks of male Officers and Noncommissioned Officers. It didn't take long to realize that my performance reviews were higher when I smiled compliantly and batted my eyes. I watched a handful of my female colleagues—who spoke their minds and stood up to blatant sexism—receive much poorer marks. An ugly lesson well learned.

Violation of Service

I can patch a sucking chest wound, apply tourniquets, call in an AEROVAC, build a tent hospital and wire it for electricity... but, I'm most prized for my abilities to make copies, un-jam printers, answer phones, and stroke egos. In the aftermath of Hurricane Katrina, I deployed to New Orleans for disaster relief. Every possible skill was called into action, and I proudly rose to the full height of my military training. Day and night, I toiled alongside fellow military members. I won awards and was lauded for humanitarian efforts, yet my male colleagues still insisted I take care of their menial secretarial tasks.

My first overseas TDY (temporary duty) was to RAF Lakenheath (Royal Air Force Base). I barely had two years of service under my belt. At the time, I was a bright-eyed English major who couldn't wait to watch a Shakespearean play at the most famous theatre in the world. As I boarded the C-130 to cross the Atlantic, a resounding chorus rang out amongst my male colleagues. "Yeah, baby!" they hollered and high-fived. "What goes TDY stays TDY!" Rather than preparing for an international training mission, they acted as though we were headed to Las Vegas.

Within a few years of completing that training mission, I once again found myself in England, near RAF Lakenheath.

One particularly nefarious NCO took special interest in ensuring that I had a memorable time. Turns out, I remember it so well that—to this day—I still feel ill when I hear any song by Depeche Mode. He had the word "Violator" tattooed on the back of his neck. Suffice it to say, he did not exemplify the Air Force Core Values of *integrity first, service before self, and excellence in all we do*. His *assistance* in making this trip memorable proved cruel and exacting. With words as sharp as a scalpel and hands as unfeeling as a butcher, he left me a shell of my former self.

In an attempt to escape his tyrannous grasp, I self-medicated by riding trains back and forth from Cambridge to London. "Mind the Gap" therapy, I like to call it, where no one looks you in the eye or has any desire to start a conversation. Alone I sat, shouldering the burdens of heavy thoughts and the weight of my soul. Even now, when I close my eyes, I can still feel the rocking motion of the train car that cradled my bruised heart. On tough days, the engine's whirring lullaby still softly sings in my ears. There are times, while walking through a crowded city, when I am overcome by a distinct smell that instantly transports me back to the train stations dotting London's Underground. That noxious mixture of exhaust, refuse, and heat is overwhelming. In those moments, I am caught completely unaware and stop dead in my tracks, but only for a minute. Without fail and with great purpose, I place one foot in front of the other. I am not a slave to my past.

I found myself in the heart of London after one such train ride. As soft snow caught in my lashes and on my wooly scarf, I found shelter in Westminster Abbey. It just so happened to be Easter Sunday. I took my seat as the service began, surrounded by hundreds of years of history. While I can't quite remember the Archbishop of Canterbury's exact words, I distinctly remember the overwhelming feeling of peace and hope that welled up deep within my broken places. I was met with a magnificent ringing of bells when I stepped back out into that snowy morning. At that point, I knew my present darkness wouldn't last forever; I discovered an unshakable strength to endure every circumstance.

Purposed to Serve

Over a decade later, I still find stumbling blocks beneath these combat boots. At nearly every Veterans' event I attend, I get asked the same question, "Oh, is your husband in the military?" Men and women alike automatically assume I am the Veteran's wife. My usual response is a good-natured smile accompanied with, "No, just me!" Yet those words—"just me"—don't do justice to the invaluable efforts of female Veterans across this country. *Just me?* As if my service is worth a fraction of a man's. *Just me?* As if lugging around a breast pump in my chem-gear bag is anything less than Herculean. Honoring the commitment of service before self takes on a whole new meaning after becoming a mother.

For almost two decades, I've endured ceaseless unwanted male attention peppered with verbal harassment at the hands of my Air Force brethren. In the midst of it all, I've worked twice as hard in order to be taken seriously. The wounds my soul endured year after year began to take their toll, and cynicism altered my naturally upbeat personality. My turning point came in the midst of a dimly lit theatre in Fort Worth, Texas. As I watched a Veteran tell his story through a powerful performance, I sat transfixed and utterly undone. Something broke open within me and came spilling out as I sat alone in the front row. My own story welled up from the depths, crying out to be heard. I met Stephan Wolfert, my Veteran mentor, after his transformative performance of *Cry Havoc*. He invited me to participate in his nonprofit program, De-Cruit, that treats military trauma through Shakespeare and research-based science. He proposes that all Veterans had a recruiter to guide them into military service, but the lack of a "de-cruiter" makes the transition into civilian life rather difficult. This phenomenal program allows Veterans to share their military experiences through story and performance; I have found there is powerful healing in storytelling. Stephan changed my entire outlook when he helped me realize my story is worth telling. That experience allowed me to see the importance of finding community among those who understand what it's like to have served. Having a safe place to share stories and speak my truth is a salve that soothes the moral injuries I've long ignored. For this reason, I encourage every Veteran to find an outlet and check out www.decruit.

org. It provided me the courage to own my story and give it its proper place.

I boldly stood center stage in a theatre filled with supportive Veterans and caring civilian audience members. Heart racing and blood pumping with excitement, I firmly planted my feet and took several deep breaths to calm my body's reaction to the spotlight. Unwaveringly, I shared my story for the first time. Woven throughout my very personal dialogue were meaningful lines from William Shakespeare. It was empowering beyond all explanation. This metamorphic moment afforded me the opportunity to spread my wings, to shed the toughened skin that accompanied the cynicism and distrust. With the final words of my performance, a physical, mental, and emotional weight was lifted from my body. Storytelling provided a path to freedom.

In the face of every challenging obstacle, I will continue to press on and proudly serve my country. As retirement looms large on my horizon, my gaze is fixed on finishing strong. Faith in my Creator, support from my family, and friendships found in fellow Veterans and concerned citizens sustains me. The uniform I wear will never be a burden to me, just as being female will never be a burden. On the contrary, they are sources of my deepest honor. In the words of Shakespeare's Hamlet, I "bear the whips and scorns of time, Th' oppressor's wrong, the proud man's contumely," for those who serve alongside me. I will stand tall among the ranks of thousands of my Camouflaged Sisters; I will carry their standard when they are too tired and weak to continue. I will be a beacon for those who feel lost at sea, drifting alone in dark waters. May my truth bear witness to our shared story of service, and may you find courage to boldly speak your truth. You are not alone. Your story matters.

SHATTERED DREAMS

☆ ☆ ☆ ☆ ☆

VIOLET BRANTLEY

Killing My Soul

I enlisted in the military with the mindset of excelling and retiring. But, from the moment I arrived at my unit, I became his prey. He made the duty roster and conveniently I was scheduled most days with him. He would make sexual remarks about my breasts, my body, and what he could do for me. I continuously told him that I was married and that I didn't appreciate his advances. My husband and I spoke to my Platoon Sergeant. We reported how he would talk down to me and how uncomfortable I felt. My husband had witnessed him cursing at me and threatened to kill him if he ever talked to me like that again. I couldn't tell my husband how he was making advances at me. I thought I could handle it. I was afraid because I saw how irate my husband became when he cursed at me.

I was never afforded the opportunity to speak out and was threatened by my Platoon Sergeant. She told me that if I went to the First Sergeant or Commander, she would make life hell for me. Hell? Hell was what I was already going through.

It was early in the morning and I was on CQ duty with Sergeant X. As I was exiting the restroom, he came in and began to get aggressive. I tried to fight him to the best of my ability but to no avail. As he penetrated me, I felt like he was sucking the life out of me, second by second. The deeper he got, the more I felt like I wanted to die and that my virtue was leaving my body. The more I fought, the more pain I felt. He was stripping me of my zeal. I began to think about my grandmother and the Scripture she would always recite to me, Jeremiah 29:11—"For I know the plans I have for you, declares the LORD..." I remember asking God, "What have I done to deserve this?" How was that His plan for me? That was one of the worst days of my life. He began to choke me and told me that if I told anyone, he would kill me. How could he threaten to kill me when he was killing the core of my soul? Mind you, we had approximately three hours before someone from our unit would relieve us. I had to sit in the room crying with my assaulter taunting and threatening me. How was I going to tell my husband or family something horrific had happened to me? Would my husband go to jail for murdering Sergeant X? If I reported it to my command, would my Platoon Sergeant take his side, or would she tell the truth about our previous conversations? Would they believe me? All of those questions were running through my mind.

Shattered Life

That was the turning point of a downward spiral. I didn't know how to deal with the assault and began to go to the doctor every day to get out of the military. I couldn't tell my husband. I put makeup on the marks to cover them when I was home. I didn't want him to go to jail. This was so unfair to me because I was a damn good Soldier and always tried to treat others with respect. I felt helpless and didn't know where to turn. I withdrew from my husband and him touching me made my skin cringe. We had a loving, wholesome relationship previously and now I was withholding a secret that I allowed to torment me for years. A secret that caused our marriage to dissolve. Performing my wifely duties were like completing a chore. I would literally throw up when he tried to touch me. Deep down I knew that something was wrong because I was outwardly expressing my pain to him, yet he didn't know why.

I began to chop glass for weeks to put in the assaulter's food and coffee to tear the lining of his stomach in hopes that he would die. I was filled with hatred and thought of ways to kill him. I had never been violent yet murdering him was on the forefront of my mind.

I grew up in a loving Christian family and had been taught forgiveness, yet the one time I needed to exercise it, I couldn't. I didn't know nor did I realize that me harboring resentment toward my assaulter was allowing hatred to fester inside me. For years, I blamed myself for him assaulting me. I questioned how I could allow something like that to happen to me. Had I worn something provocative that would give him the notion that I was promiscuous, or was I too friendly?

I attend Christian House of Prayer, under the leadership of Apostle Nate and Pastor Valerie Holcomb, and graduated from Sonship School of the Firstborn. Over the years, Apostle has spoken numerous times on forgiveness, yet I was in denial that I had unforgiveness in my heart. I remember him saying that forgiveness wasn't for the other person, it freed you up. Immediately the light went off.

After 30 years of concealing the shame of being assaulted, I had to go back to what I had been taught as a young girl and grown lady. It was long overdue; the time had come for me to forgive myself. But I couldn't forgive myself until I forgave Sergeant X and my Platoon Sergeant. On Christmas Day 2016, a gentleman came to my house selling insurance. I asked my daughter to let him in. I was lying on the couch and he came to the foot of the couch. I looked at him and asked him his name. He told me his name was Mr. Harris and I said, "SSG Harris?" He said, "How did you know I was a Staff Sergeant?" I asked him if he knew my old Platoon Sergeant. He said, "Yes, she is my ex-wife." I jumped off the couch and began to say, "Thank You, Jesus!" Tears were flowing down my face. Everyone was looking at me like I had lost my mind. I told him I had been looking for her for over 30 years. He immediately asked me to forgive her because she had some professional difficulties at the time. He also told me that he knew something had occurred while I was in the military because I got out so abruptly. He called her on the phone and she agreed to meet with me the next week.

The day came for the meeting and she made an excuse why she couldn't meet me. She texted me saying that she remembered an incident occurring, but it was "gray" in her mind. "Gray" told me that she remembered but wanted to excuse the part that she played. Me being persistent, I went to her office to meet with her anyway. That was my day to speak out and I was going to do just that. I knew that it was time for me to truly be given the opportunity to speak and release my pain.

Forgiveness, It's for Me

She invited me into a room so that we could talk in private. She became very apologetic. I told her that this had caused me tremendous grief throughout life and that it caused me and my husband to divorce. I told her it was not fair. As our leader, she always told us that she would protect us; yet, when I needed her, she turned her back on me and sided with my assaulter. I told her that it wasn't fair and that I was a great Soldier who had a promising future and it was stolen from me. My dreams of retiring were shattered because I had no one to stand up for me legally or professionally.

I asked her how could she have seen the marks on me and that I was in distress; yet, instruct me to go home and she would take care of it? After asking her what she did with the statement I provided her about my assault, she had the unmitigated gall to say that she gave it to the First Sergeant and thought he took care of it. Mind you, this was early in 1985 and there was nothing in place for sexual harassment. In all honesty, it was a man's Army. Back then, women Soldiers weren't given the same consideration or recognition as our male counterparts. We were treated very badly.

I told her that for years I had a great deal of resentment towards her and that it was not her place to decide whether I was given an opportunity to defend myself legally or not. I told her that what happened to me and the decisions she made caused me tremendous grief throughout my life and in my relationships.

She began to get emotional and told me that the same thing had also happened to her. She wanted to spare me the humiliation that came with being assaulted and the stigma that she was plagued with. I had to reiterate to her that she literally threatened me about going to the First Sergeant and that it should have been my decision, not hers.

Although I had not been afforded the opportunity to face my assaulter, I left the meeting with my old Platoon Sergeant feeling very emotional and slightly relieved that I was able to voice my concerns. Although I still have flashbacks and nightmares about the event, I truly feel like me verbalizing it to someone who played a tremendous part in the assault gave me a sense of relief and has been one of the tools I needed to begin my recovery. Forgiveness allowed me the opportunity to begin to pick up the pieces of my life and live.

THE BATTLE IS NOT MINE

☆ ☆ ☆ ☆ ☆

SHAYLA HAWKINS

"He giveth power to the faint; and to them that have no might he increaseth strength. Even the youths shall faint and be weary, and the young men shall utterly fall:

But they that wait upon the Lord shall renew their strength; they shall mount up with wings as eagles; they shall run, and not be weary; and they shall walk, and not faint."

—*Isaiah 40:29-31 (KJV)*

Born to Serve

The thought of sharing my life with the world seemed a bit awkward, but the moment I realized that God had given me a voice and a story I knew I had to share my journey. I pray that people will be impacted in such a way that lives will be transformed, and individuals and relationships will be restored to God's initial plan and purpose. Until this point, I didn't realize I was hurting others by concealing my past troubles and triumphs and not sharing my story. When your way of living is covering up and coping, it takes a Higher Power to learn how to overcome. I finally came to terms with the fact that I couldn't be my best self by covering up and coping. It took me building a relationship with God and spending time in His presence to learn how to overcome years of sexual abuse that started at five years old; observing domestic violence and alcoholism; a life without a father; reduction in military rank; and loss to miscarriage, death, and prison. So, when people ask me, "Why are you so calm in this situation?" I simply reply, "When you have been through so much and still have the ability to stand, there is no question or doubt, you just know that all is well."

Choosing a career is one of the most important decisions we will ever make, yet many of us are forced to make that decision much earlier in life rather than later. With that being said, career decisions are made before we even know who we are. How do you know what you want to do with your life when you don't even know who you are? For me, my purpose and passion developed as I navigated through my childhood. I grew up in a multi-family household, spending most of my childhood caring for my grandmother—from cooking her meals to paying her bills. The time spent with her definitely served as an advantage as she taught me so much about God and conducting business. Most importantly, she taught me how to communicate and develop a relationship with God.

Serving my grandmother gave me such a great sense of satisfaction that I couldn't see my future beyond the age of 13 after watching her take her last breath. From that day forward, I knew that I needed to start planning for my future and I had to plan fast. For the next few years, I lived with a couple of my aunts while keeping busy with school, work, extracurricular activities, and preparing for a military career. After turning 17, I was finally able to officially serve by enlisting in the Army with parental consent. I was so excited because I just knew it would be the path to allow me to fulfill my purpose to serve.

Ambushed by the Enemy

Immediately after completing Army Basic Training, I took advantage of the academic scholarship I had received and enrolled in college and ROTC (Reserve Officers Training Corps). As I entered my senior year of college, what should have been a time of excitement and celebration quickly turned into turmoil. With just two months left in my senior year, my world began to slowly crumble. For several days, at the conclusion of PT (Physical Training), I felt nauseous. I finally went to see a doctor to learn that I was eight weeks pregnant. I didn't panic. In my mind I felt that because I was engaged and just a few weeks from graduating and commissioning as an Army Officer, everything would be just fine.

The next week I was advised by ROTC that I would not be commissioned because my security clearance had been denied. At that point, although I was feeling the pressure, I carried on with business as usual—studying for finals—hoping and praying that everything would fall into place before graduation. The week before graduation, final grades were posted and that's when I learned that I had failed a required class. At that point, I was falling apart on the inside. But I had to hold it together since I had already submitted my graduation application, ordered my cap and gown, and invited family to the graduation.

As Soldiers, we are trained to mask our true feelings, suck it up, and carry on. I had been so good at doing all of those things before even joining the military, but this time things were different. For the first time, I felt that my life was crumbling right before me. For the first time, I didn't have answers and it was all just too much. Everything around me became so cloudy that it was hard for me to see myself getting through the situation.

After faking it through graduation, I made arrangements with my professor to take my class over. I contacted the ROTC to see what was required to request an appeal for my security clearance, but things just weren't working out in my favor. Several months after graduation, I delivered a baby girl and was married. I then learned that my husband of only a few months was facing a one-year prison sentence. In the midst of the turmoil, I began to learn things about myself that I never knew. I had gotten so used to doing everything on my own that I wasn't relying on God for anything. When I reached the point where I had exhausted all of my own efforts, I learned how to be silent and just listen.

My God-given talents and abilities began to surface. Even though deep down I felt sad and alone, God had given me the ability to motivate and encourage others. Even though I was going through, God continued to put people before me that just needed encouragement. That's when I learned that regardless of what's going on in life, you cannot just shut down. There are so many hurting people that need to be nurtured and restored. We must recognize when we need nurturing so that we are strong enough to nurture others.

The Mission Must Continue

At that point in my life, I was so ashamed of all of the events that had taken place in the previous months. Although I had received my degree, the security clearance and commission situation were still unresolved. I didn't even have the energy to address it because I was so stressed about my husband going to prison, leaving me with an infant to care for. To avoid my unit leaders' questions about my commission, I would call off from going to weekend drill. I did this for almost a year. My unit leaders wanted answers about my commission status. My Commander advised me that since I had not received my commission, they were forced to reduce my rank from a Cadet to an E-4 Specialist.

That was the point in my military career when I felt like I wanted to give up. Becoming a Commissioned Officer was something that I had worked so hard for, I couldn't accept that it wasn't going to happen. But, it's times like those when we must accept that God might have completely different plans for us.

Navigating the Soul

At that point, I had to make a decision that would impact my family for life. I had to dig deep and spend time with God. Every time I prayed about it, I was reminded of the places I would go and the people I would meet. As I reminisced, I realized I hadn't gone very many places and I hadn't met very many people. The real question that needed to be answered was would I conform to the world and cancel out God's promise?

I contacted my unit and advised them that I would be at the next drill weekend with my reduced rank. They informed me that I would be transferring to a new unit that would be closer to my home where I would be working in an entirely different arena. Although I was disappointed about my commission, there was relief in knowing that I wouldn't have to explain my situation to every person in my old unit.

I reported to my new Command, which was Officer heavy, with my E-4 rank on and to my surprise they instantly embraced me and my administrative skills. Within a few months, I was promoted to E-5 and received a hefty reenlistment bonus. I could feel that I was lining back up with my life's purpose. There are times when we are faced with so many obstacles that we get off course. Navigate your way back into God's presence and align yourself with the plan and purpose God has for your life. Never be swift to make life-long decisions based on a temporary place. It only takes one thing, word, or person to change your entire situation.

More than a Conqueror

In my new assignment, I worked in the commandant's office—providing administrative support to senior officers, and planning and facilitating trainings and conferences all over the world. The chief of staff was impressed with the level of support I provided and offered me a full-time Human Resource position within the command. Over the next seven years, I was able to build relationships that remain invaluable to this very day. None of the things I am doing today are remotely close to the lifestyle I came from. We are often told to just deal with whatever comes in life. Today, I am telling you to address the issues so that you can find true healing.

BEYOND THE RANKS— LIFE REIMAGINED

☆ ☆ ☆ ☆ ☆

DONNA NEWMAN-ROBINSON

I Soon Realized

I served on Active Duty in the US Army from 1980-2000. I experienced two unique transitions while serving 10 years as an enlisted Soldier in the Army medical department and the remaining 10 years as a commissioned officer in the Army Nurse Corps. It was a different time for me, and for military women during those days. The occupational specialties were limited and there were less women serving than there are today. I was afforded many opportunities from a supportive chain of command; however, my personal life became more difficult to manage. It seemed like each time I was promoted to the next higher rank, my personal life was demoted and out of control.

When I joined the military, I was married but separated from my first husband and had my first child. I also had been working as a licensed practical nurse at the time. The marriage was heading to divorce when I reported to Basic Training at Fort Dix, New Jersey, in January of 1980. Although I was new to the military way of life, I was not a young recruit arriving to my new duty station.

I remember my first experience in learning what was required to be successful in the military. I was an E-3, working as a 91C, Army Practical Nurse, in the newborn nursery/postpartum ward at the Fort Stewart hospital in MEDDAC (Medical Department Activity). I had six years of nursing experience before the military, so when I worked with an Army Nurse Corps Captain, I soon realized that I had more experience than her. However, I was not recognized for that because I was just a Private First Class (PFC).

I became frustrated very often working with this nurse officer who was lazy and abused her status with me. Of course, I did not take that very well. So much so, that without thinking about military customs or courtesy, I called the nursing office and complained to the Chief Nurse of the hospital. Yes, this older, more experienced, E-3, 91C, called and complained to the Chief Nurse, a Colonel, about one of her nurses! Thankfully, I did not get in any trouble because my complaints were legitimate. I made up my mind then that in order to be recognized for my skills and nursing experience, I needed to become a Nurse Corps officer!

On a Mission

I researched what was required to obtain that goal. I needed to have a bachelor's degree in nursing first. I had all the information and resources available to me to make that happen. However, it wasn't meant to happen that soon. Life got in the way. By that, I mean, I had divorced my first husband by then, and had met my future second husband. I married my second husband and had my second child a year later. I arrived at my next duty station with a new husband and now two young daughters.

We were stationed overseas in Germany. My new husband was still Active Duty at the time. I was assigned to a great unit that supported my goals of becoming a Nurse Corps officer. While I was being groomed for that career goal, my husband's career was floundering. He became a rebellious and unhappy Soldier. He elected to not reenlist for present duty station, so he separated at the end of his enlistment and became a dependent husband. It was the beginning of a life I never thought I would survive.

My chain of command was made aware of the tumultuous incidences occurring because these incidences involved the military police and other law enforcement agencies while serving overseas. I remember my Company Commander telling me one day, "I will do whatever I can to keep your husband from ruining your career, even if I have him sent back to the States." Although I was relieved to know that, I declined his support in making that happen. I wanted my marriage to work because I loved my husband and my family.

Mission Accomplished

My next duty location was Fort Sam Houston, Texas. I was assigned to instructor duty at AMEDD (Army Medical Department) Combat Medical Specialist Division. I was so focused on moving forward with my career goals that once situated in my new assignment as an instructor, I enrolled in college courses that would transfer and inevitably be accepted into the University of Texas Health Science Center School of Nursing program. Meanwhile, the drama of marriage woes picked up again.

Yes!

Things became more dangerous, more unpredictable, and more out of control. During my time as an instructor, I was the only female in my section of 10-12 instructors (maybe more). I became the little sister to those male instructors with whom I worked closely. I confided in them about my problems at home. It became so bad at times that my team leaders would call me on a Sunday, prior to the work week, to check in to see if I was ok. We had a system in place. If they called and I answered the phone, it was very brief. "You ok?" "Yes, I'm ok." It became so bad that if they saw me in public with my husband, they knew not to acknowledge me for fear of the consequences when we got home.

While all of that was going on, I stayed focused on my career goal to obtain my degree and get my commission. I thought, "If I get that far, I'm divorcing this abusive, insecure, controlling man." So, I endured the turmoil. My chain of command was supportive and believed in me, a good Soldier who was trying to do my best despite all the obstacles. As I got closer to my career goals and was accepted into my nursing program, I had to change my work hours to complete required courses. So, I decided to leave the instructor platform and was reassigned to Brooke Army Medical Center. That transition was successful but not easy because I had to work night shifts in order to perform clinical hours during the day.

Somewhere in between all of that, my husband wanted another child. I believe he felt that if I was burdened down with another child, it would slow me down in accomplishing my goal. Well, it didn't. I had my third daughter, continued to deal with his abusive behavior, and stayed focused on my goal. It seemed the more determined I became, the worse he became. It's hard to believe I stayed through it all.

I graduated on time, received my commission, separated from the US Army one day, and commissioned in the US Army Nurse Corps the next day. I was still married to the same husband. I believe he sensed that my plan was to divorce him once my goals were accomplished. At that time, he apologized profusely for all his wrongdoing and I forgave him… again, like an idiot.

If I Survived

Things were going smoothly for a while, until our second assignment overseas to Germany. This time as an officer, as well as with a fourth daughter. Once again, my chain of command stepped in with advice and guidance. I was getting close to thinking about my retirement and how I visualized my life to be after military service. *If I survived.*

I knew in my heart that this was not how I wanted to live my life. Pressing through to retire to receive my military retirement pension and benefits became my biggest motivator. *If I survived.*

Things were beginning to take shape in that endeavor. I sought out counseling from mental health professionals and my church family. That gave me the strength to start the process of ending the abusive relationship. I knew once I started there was no going back. I also knew he was not going to make it easy. *If I survived.*

Well, as you can see, **I did survive.** My military career saved my life. My military experience taught me that I possessed internal strength,

it taught me sacrifice,

it taught me resiliency,

it taught me courage, and

it taught me how to be a leader in my life.

As a woman Veteran and baby boomer, that life experience has made me the woman I am today. It created a life reimagined with endless possibilities and opportunities to live on my own terms.

AN EFFECTIVE CHANGE AGENT

☆ ☆ ☆ ☆ ☆

JOYCE V. HAMILTON

Never Give Up

I was born and raised in Brooklyn, New York, and hit rock bottom in my life. I was trying to escape from a very physically, mentally, and emotionally abusive relationship. As a result, I lived in a life of poverty and homelessness with two small children at the age of 19. I lived in an abandoned building with two small children, ages one and newborn, for one year with a mattress on the floor, a cat to keep the rats away, and my door was not even on the hinges.

Something inside of me rose up and said, "I don't know how I got here living like this, but I don't want to stay here." I prayed to God to help me get out of that broken place because I had something great to offer society and deserved to live better than where I was. I would think about my life and remembered that I was skipped from the seventh to the ninth grade, graduated from high school early, and had administrative skills.

I wanted a permanent solution in my life, not a temporary fix of living with other people or moving from one home to another. I wanted an open-door opportunity. I heard a still, small voice in my spirit that said, "Go into the military." I began to pursue this opportunity. I went to see every recruiter from every branch of service, and stated to myself, "The branch of service who accepts me first is the one I will select to begin my journey to a new life." The Army answered the call right away. I passed all my tests. The Army recruiter came to my abandoned building where I was staying, took my children to my mother's home (she would serve as their guardian), and I was off to Basic Training at Fort Dix, New Jersey, on my youngest daughter's first birthday, November 5, 1985.

I remember going down to the welfare office prior to leaving for Basic Training. With my shoulders held high, I proudly looked them in the eyes letting them know I would no longer need their services because I was about to be a Soldier in the US Army. I walked out of the welfare office and NEVER looked back.

As my military career progressed, I was given opportunities to work in positions of greater responsibility, authority, and leadership. At that time in my life, I was once again a single parent—of four young children now—divorced twice, no child support, and in charge of many Soldiers and civilians. It was very challenging to financially manage my household, robbing Peter to pay Paul for my entire military career. I was engaged in my children's educational and personal lives to the max, making sure that they were at child care and school on time. I was getting myself to Physical Training (PT) formations very early in the morning, and I was the first to arrive at the office and the last one out. I was always making sure that everyone else was taken care of. I have many Army stories to share after 22 years of Active Duty service, but some in particular stand out the most. They can help others become effective change agents who never give up and maintain integrity no matter what.

Maintain My Integrity

I remember when I was a Drill Sergeant (DS) from 1996-1999. I was the ONLY female DS in that unit in 1997. The Drill Sergeants were not ready for a female in the unit and would walk around in their underwear. My bathroom door did not have a lock, and male trainees would walk in on me while I was showering. The First Sergeant and Drill Sergeants shared the belief that they didn't have to change for me. It was a horrible unit. I witnessed Drill Sergeants out of shape, not properly training Troops, forging PT test scores, hazing Privates by having them pull their pants down, and threatening trainees the DS said had contraband.

As an ethical standard bearer, I was hated by my peers for wanting to do what was right. I was not in a clique and stood alone. It got so bad that my rater tried to give me a bad NCOER, and I refused to accept it. I went to talk to the First Sergeant and Commander but got no help because they were all in on trying to ruin my military career. I then went to the Inspector General's (IG's) office and shared what I had experienced and what the trainees were going through. I discovered that the IG's office was trying to figure out why there were so many negative complaints already from that unit. I didn't know what would happen, but it became a very hostile working environment for me, and the IG moved me out of that unit until the investigation was over.

Wives of the Drill Sergeants under investigation called cursing me out and there was evil all around me. My strong faith in God kept me grounded. I believed I would prevail and be victorious, knowing that righteousness outweighs any wrong. I listened to the song, "The Battle is Not Yours," by Yolanda Adams daily in order to stay focused. The IG's office interviewed all my trainees, and they shared that I was the best DS in the unit. The investigation was substantiated. All the Drill Sergeants who were abusing their authority, lying, etcetera were reprimanded.

I was moved out of that unhealthy unit to another organization where I was able to lead effectively without backlash. After my first training cycle in my new unit, I won Drill Sergeant of the Cycle for my merits and abilities. I was promoted to Sergeant First Class, the only one selected in the unit. I was considered a trailblazer who paved the way for other female Drill Sergeants, even causing policies and procedures to be changed. I was overwhelmed with joy when new female Drill Sergeants arrived at the unit and stated that they had heard all about me and thanked me for paving the way for them. If I had to do it all over again, I would.

I would say, it's inside of me; I was born a positive change agent. The Lord has given me the ability to stand up and not tolerate injustice against those who cannot fight for themselves. I was selected by the Post Command Sergeant Major to become a Drill Sergeant Leader and teach at the Drill Sergeant School because of my integrity, physical fitness standards, and professionalism.

Another impactful position I served in was as an Equal Opportunity Advisor (EOA) for five consecutive years while deployed to Iraq, then while assigned to Fort Benning, Georgia, and Fort Knox, Kentucky. Those assignments allowed me to engage Soldiers daily to find out how they were being treated in their units. I served as the eyes and ears of the Brigade Commander while advocating for Soldiers and civilians and working to create healthy working environments for all to succeed. I was able to just be myself, maintain my integrity, and express personal courage as I addressed issues of racism, sexism, and sexual harassment at all levels of leadership. Being a Drill Sergeant, Drill Sergeant Leader, and Equal Opportunity Advisor set me up for success in my civilian federal job after retirement. The positions I served in allowed me to master the special skill of courage to face negative opposition and at the same time be approachable for many who knew their concerns would be heard and nothing would be swept under the rug.

Still Serving

I retired from the US Army in December 2007 and worked diligently and consistently from January 2008 until May 2019 for the US Army Wounded Warrior Program (AW2). I retired on May 9, 2019, after a total of 34 years of federal service. I worked as an AW2 advocate (my job title) for seriously injured, ill, and wounded Soldiers, and family members and caregivers on Fort Knox, Kentucky. My clients had injuries such as loss of limbs, chronic post-traumatic stress disorder, traumatic brain injuries, paralysis, blindness, hearing loss, burns, and limited life expectancy. I ensured my clients would have a smooth transition to civilian life, empowered them, and linked them to every agency that would provide them with their benefits and entitlements. Now after 34 years of federal service, I am still advocating for our most vulnerable population—low income, poverty stricken, homeless patrons in our local community that others may forget. It's in my blood and DNA to advocate for those who are less fortunate, those who find it difficult to help themselves, and those who have lost hope.

I find joy by serving in our community alongside my phenomenal husband, a 20-year retired US Army Veteran himself. Since May 2013, we have owned and operated our non-profit, 501c3, The Lord's Supper Soup Kitchen Mobile Ministry, advocating and feeding the hungry and homeless in our community. Our motto is to "FEED, LEAD, and FUL-FILL the NEED." We travel in our RV to neighborhoods with the most needs, low income and impoverished, and love on them by providing a hot meal to a large number of homeless and hungry patrons. My husband and I sing gospel music the entire time, pray for them, and minister the Word of God. We also provide basic need items like food or snack bags, clothing, shoes, toys, and household items. All from donations and volunteers helping us with our outreach and mission programs. It is such a blessing and reward to be retired from the US Army but still serve while maintaining my integrity, never giving up, and being an effective change agent.

"But by the grace of God I am what I am."

—*1 Corinthians 15:10 (KJV)*

ARMY BRAT, AIR FORCE SPOUSE, AND EVERYTHING IN BETWEEN!

☆ ☆ ☆ ☆ ☆

SHARON FINNEY

So Many Titles

Between 2012 and 2015, I accumulated a series of magnets for my car. One was Army mom after my oldest son joined the Army Reserves as a college freshman. A month later, my youngest son entered the Army's delayed entry program, which meant he would be a Soldier shortly after graduating high school. Before long, I was back at the store getting an Air Force wife magnet. My husband of eight and a half years decided to return to the Air Force in a part-time capacity. "Cool! I think I could adjust to the military spouse life!" The last magnet for this camouflage collage—Air Force mom.

Yes, it's true. I am an Army Veteran and Army brat, but my baby girl chose the Air Force. Hey, no complaint here. I jokingly stated that she chose this way in order to wear earrings with her camouflage. Back in my day, Army women only wore earrings with our class A and B uniforms.

When I had my three magnets displayed proudly on my car, a dear friend reminded me that I was a Veteran. I didn't even notice I had nothing displayed to acknowledge my own military service, though I have keychains and caps representing my branch of service and two deployments. I am a proud Veteran, and of course, I will never forget that fact. But for some reason, I found myself enamored as I boasted of these new affiliations by my family members who are serving.

My life has been full of military encounters. When I grew up as the daughter of a career Soldier, the Army brat was exposed to a high level of discipline. My father had many nicknames which alluded to his passion for soldiering. He was known for highly spit shined boots and his small physique, with a voice that commanded the utmost respect. A few words would bring an entire room to attention, and he always went above and beyond the call of duty. I guess my first magnet should have been an olive drab green one with black, stenciled letters reading, "Army Brat." This truly was the only life I knew from birth until age 17 when Dad retired.

My senior year of high school introduced change. I just started at a new high school, as many military kids were known to do. I felt my future plans (even though they were not firm) had to be reworked since I was attending a different school in a new state, far from what was familiar. On a whim, I took the ASVAB which meant a recruiter had a conversation with me. When the somewhat seasoned, yet unknowing sergeant showed up at our house, my father scared him away. He informed the recruiter that "my daughter will not be enlisting in the Army." But why in the world wouldn't the career Soldier allow this? I was taken aback, but I proceeded on with deciding another pathway. Changing plans was not optional because Dad was firm with his decisions. He was not going to let me enlist for Army band consideration. I had to do something else. The continued love for music and band was evident. Still wanting to do something in this field led me to the college planning experience. This is when I decided to attend college for a music degree.

When I arrived on campus, becoming an Army officer was furthest from my mind. But somehow, I found myself enrolling in ROTC while selecting my freshman classes. As soon as I was issued a uniform, I wanted to show my family, especially Dad! Mom wondered if I was serious about this ROTC thing. She knew of my thoughts to join the Army band, but this path would not afford me such an opportunity. One weekend, I made my way home for a short visit. With great excitement, I unpacked all my gear. This was the last year of fatigues for Army ROTC Cadets. I tried on my pickle suit so Mom could take a picture of me with her Polaroid camera. Afterwards, I hung up my uniform and made my way to the front porch with boots in hand, some cotton balls, a tin of Kiwi polish, a newspaper, and an old T-shirt. I almost got laughed out of the neighborhood while attempting to put a spit shine on those new boots. My efforts to mimic what I observed from childhood came as a surprise to Dad, for unbeknown to him, his baby girl was watching closely. It was evident that I had not mastered his technique, but I knew the components of his process. We ended up rescuing my boots as a team. He had one boot, and I had the other.

Being a first-generation college kid, it was imperative that I finish what I started. I struggled with some decisions, but eventually learned to accept things and keep pressing forward. My heart wanted to go to the Army Band, but I sort of felt as though I settled on the degree and ROTC path. Some may find it strange that I use this choice of words to describe my experience, but this is my truth. When I took the ASVAB as a high school senior, I thought perhaps I'd enlist specifically to serve in the band. My plan was to do at least one tour, then consider going to college for a music degree. I just didn't feel college ready while dealing with my new high school. Every other idea that crossed my teenage mind involved pathways outside of a college campus. I don't regret pursuing and ultimately obtaining my degree in music, but at the same time, I often wondered what could have been had I earned a place in one of the Army bands.

Upon graduation, I entered active military service. I was exposed to a wealth of experiences which taught me valuable lessons to carry with me in future assignments, military or civilian. Although I would depart from military service after becoming a mom, I found my way back as a Reserve Officer, giving four more years to Uncle Sam. After all of that, I just didn't anticipate ever being connected to the military again. But my path led back towards the military in other ways, including Army contractor and Army civilian.

Who Is the Veteran Anyway?

Recently, I saw a T-shirt advertisement with the following slogan as one of their new pieces, "I'm the Veteran, not the Veteran's wife!" I smiled when I first saw it, but my reality is, "I am the Veteran AND the Veteran's wife!" I am one of many spouses who separated from military service, but I possess an ID card. Others like me are classified as dependents. As shared in the book, *Behind the Rank, Volume 1*, I got out without retiring from the military. I commissioned twice (yes, that is possible) and separated from the Army for good after my second deployment. Leaving my children again was not an option. I was a divorced mother juggling the realities and demands of my unique situation, and the whole experience took a toll on me, my children, and our support systems. I eventually remarried. Twelve years after becoming a civilian, I found myself cheering on my husband, the man who after ten years away from his branch of service chose to pick up where he left off.

So, at the blink of an eye, we became a military family. I was actually a military spouse, a dependent, and a card-carrying member of this exclusive club! Although I didn't know a whole lot about the Air National Guard, I was excited for my husband's decision and what was to come. His last military experience was a year or so before we met. Through the years, I'd seen his photos from assignments, so I had a point of reference. We even had old uniforms in the basement that we glanced at when feeling nostalgic. I tried to learn more about what made his branch so different than mine. I worked in one joint assignment during my career, so again, my Air Force knowledge was limited. This doesn't keep us from having our dialogs on military topics.

I always felt very welcomed engaging in activities that included spouses. Whenever my schedule allowed, I tried my best to participate. For the most part, many had no idea I was a Veteran. I just didn't see a reason to randomly bring it up, but situations have a way of presenting themselves. At his promotion ceremony, my husband took a moment to acknowledge me and gave a little of my background. When he stated that I was an Army Veteran and former commissioned officer, some eyebrows raised. I know that for quite a few guests, it was their first time hearing that. Those who follow me on social media were not surprised because I would proudly post something related to my service on Veterans Day, usually a throwback picture in my beret and battle dress uniform.

I will occasionally compare my mother's life as a military spouse to my own. There are obvious differences since her generation had many stay-at-home moms. As a military spouse, she participated in groups like the NCO Wives Club. I remember attending family-oriented events hosted by their club, ripping the runway as I modeled the latest back-to-school fashions at the annual show. Needless to say, I did my part in representing my family for events such as those. The family support groups of today differ greatly as many spouses are employed, and some are Veterans. Activities may be similar, but members come with diverse backgrounds personally and professionally.

Are there challenges with being a Veteran while also supporting my husband in his military endeavors? Yes and no. Perhaps because I have separated from military service, it does occasionally bring forth feelings of missing out, or wanting to chime in on topics, situations, and circumstances. But for the most part, I am mindful of the fact that my time has passed. Though at times, I feel my knowledge and experience could be helpful, it isn't my place nor my duty to volunteer suggestions in situations which don't concern me. I have to simply stay in my lane!

QUALIFIED, EVEN WHEN I DIDN'T BELIEVE I WAS

☆ ☆ ☆ ☆ ☆

SAMANTHA JEAN JASSO

Physically Qualified

I joined the Army by faith. It was never a goal, dream, or back-up plan of mine to join the military. Even though I struggled, I am thankful that I served. To be honest, I didn't think I was going to make it through Basic Training, AIT (Advanced Individual Training), and my duty station. Once I got to my duty station, I didn't think I was going to be there for more than a year. I was scared that I would fail. I really didn't want anybody to know that I signed up for the Army. Although I was afraid to fail, I believed I was supposed to join the Army.

I had been at my duty station for a while and we were told that we were going to have an eight-mile ruck march that we had to complete within two hours and thirty minutes. If we did not meet the standards, we would have to do it over again until we could accomplish it in the time frame. I was angry when I learned that information.

Why was I angry? I felt like I was told at the last minute that the march was going to count, and I did not feel like I was prepared for it. I was not mentally ready, I hadn't eaten well the night before nor had I eaten breakfast before the ruck march, and I didn't get a good night's rest. The truth is, I had the wrong mindset when I was told about the ruck march. I should have always been prepared for a ruck march, whether it was practice or not. What I had lost sight of too was that we were preparing to go to war. The enemy does not care if we are prepared to do something or not; we need to be ready and give it all we got, no matter what.

After I had learned that the ruck march was going to count, my attitude was, "I am going to fail." When the ruck march began, I didn't try. Why didn't I try? I believed that I was going to fail. I looked at my watch during the march and found that I was actually doing good! Despite the lack of mental preparedness, food, and sleep, I was doing it! I was so excited! Despite developing a blister on my heel and feeling it pop while I was marching, I made it in two hours and twenty-eight minutes. Was I the fastest person in the company?

No. What matters is that I did it and made it on time. All I needed was to believe in myself.

Weapon Qualified

Basic Training was the first time I fired a weapon. I struggled to qualify. I was so overwhelmed when I was at Basic Training that I was afraid to ask questions about how a weapon works and what I could do to improve. I didn't understand anything. It was a miracle that I graduated from Basic Training. After several years at my duty station, I accomplished something with my weapon at the indoor range. When we got to the range, once again my mindset was, "I am going to fail." I thought, "How many times am I going to have to do this today?" I never believed that I would get any better with the weapon than I was in Basic Training. So, you can imagine my shock when I hit 38 out of 40 targets! I felt so good! I was so excited that I had someone take my picture with my paper targets! When I looked at the picture, it kind of reminded me of a little girl holding up her artwork. LOL.

When I achieved those two accomplishments, I received mixed responses. Some people were supportive. Others made comments about how happy I was because I usually wasn't happy like that. But then again, why wouldn't I be at that moment? Still, others responded with smart remarks such as, "They were not moving targets" or "I shot 40 out of 40." Why couldn't I just have my moments and people be happy for me?

Qualified to ETS

My first day in the Army was January 4, 2012. My last day in the Army was March 16, 2016. I actually did it! I didn't think I could. I didn't believe I could. If you were to go to the town I graduated high school from and the town that I graduated college from and ask people who knew me if they would have ever thought that I would join the Army and serve as long as I did, many would say no. I would say no myself.

I got out of the Army because of depression and anxiety. Could I have maybe fought to stay in? Yes. But did I want to, no. I do not regret serving. It was not meant for me to serve in the Army for a long time.

Still Qualified

Being a Service Member and being out of the Army for three years has prepared me to help people who want to be in the military, are in the military, are transitioning out of the military, and are out of the military. While I worked at the Veteran Resource Center (VRC), I gave available referrals to Service Members, Veterans, and their family members to help meet their needs such as employment, shelter, housing, food, clothing, financial help, and counseling. On Tuesdays, I would take clients from the VRC and we would all participate in equine therapy at Horse Play at Mesquite Ranch in Amarillo, Texas. On Thursdays, I would facilitate or co-facilitate a peer-to-peer support group (Bring Everyone In The Zone). Sometimes Veterans came to the VRC because all they wanted was someone to listen to them. And that is what I did, I listened.

During the last year I was in the military and since I have been out, I volunteer to help with Patton Veterans Project at least once a year. It is a short film workshop for Veterans that enables participants to collaborate with peers to process their service experiences. I participated in the workshop while I was stationed at Fort Drum.

Since January 2018, I serve as an administrator for the Facebook page: Veteran 2 Hire. I post information about job openings, resumes and cover letters, job interview tips, and employment opportunities available for Service Members, Veterans, and their family members. I have also shared about my mental health struggles to encourage others.

Qualified to Connect

I want to share one more story. It demonstrates being qualified and having a purpose, despite a lack of experience. It happened while I was working at the Veteran Resource Center.

There is very little traffic in the VRC after 5:00 p.m., but the center doesn't close until 8:00 p.m., in case someone can't come to the center until later. One day after 5:00 p.m., a guy around my age came into the center. It was his first time in the center. I could tell that the guy was going through something. I could feel it. He was a Special Forces Veteran, a community that I am not a part of.

I don't remember exactly what I told him, but I let him know that I cared and that he was welcome to come to the center when it's open. I believe in prayer and I was led to pray for the guy when I got home. I got on my knees and prayed to God to help him. I didn't believe I would see him anymore.

When I went to work the next day, I was excited that he came back to the center to use the computers. I don't remember how our conversations got started, but we talked about towns and cities that have different military and Veteran organizations, and our experiences with losing someone we knew to suicide, amongst other things. Even though I wasn't a part of his community and I didn't deploy like he had, I could relate to being a part of the military and a Veteran. Because of that, we were qualified to connect.

You Are Qualified

If you are in the military, you are qualified to be there. Do what you are supposed to do and do not let yourself or others make you feel like you are not qualified to be there. It's ok to struggle to qualify, but you have to believe that you can qualify. Do not let yourself stay stuck in your struggle or you may find yourself disqualified to stay in the military. You may fall but you have to get back up again.

If you are thinking about joining the military and you qualify, you can do it. I was unable to make the volleyball team in middle school and was at the bottom of my JV tennis team in high school, but I served in the US Army honorably for a little more than four years. Prior to the military, I never fired a weapon; yet, when I was in, I shot 38 out of 40. So, yes you can.

Even if you have no desire to join the military, you are qualified for something. Everybody has a purpose. It may take a while to figure out what your purpose is, but you have one.

FROM PAIN TO PERSEVERANCE

☆ ☆ ☆ ☆ ☆

IASHA K. NICHOLS

Overcome Violence

I realize now that my will to persevere began long before I joined the military, as I dealt with teen dating violence at the ages of 14 and 15. That is something I will never forget. For me to cope with it all, I would say to myself, "He didn't mean it," "I made him upset," and "I know this is the last time it will happen." But that was simply not the case, as the abuse continued until I mustered up the strength to say never again and mean it. I forgave quickly and accepted the many apologies, just for things to get worse.

Can you imagine being hit in the face with a 2x4 or having a gun held to your head at that age? Well, some of you may be able to relate while others not so much. I hope it is the latter for you all. I knew that I did not deserve that type of treatment, but I did not break away until I was emotionally strong enough to do so. For some reason, I stayed in that toxic situation for approximately two years, crying when I was alone and pretending to be ok when I truly wasn't. In some way, that eventually gave me the strength to leave and never look back. I hid that from everyone in my family simply because I did not want any issues on either side. There was something within me that changed forever when all of that happened to me and it has affected me my whole life. So, if you are experiencing this or have in the past, be empowered. Find your strength—your will and your voice—so that you do not suffer any longer. You will persevere!

According to the Center for Disease Control and Prevention, "teen dating violence can be physical, emotional, or sexual and includes stalking. It can occur in person or electronically, which includes texting, social media, and other online applications." As this abuse is widespread and has serious long-term and short-term effects, many teens do not report it because they are simply afraid to do so. Source: https://www.cdc.gov/features/DatingViolence/

Let's educate and empower our children so that they do not endure this type of emotional and physical pain! They will persevere!

Overcome Betrayal

Later as a Soldier, my trust was shattered into pieces at the hands of the same people I was to trust with everything, including my life. These same people brought about fear, panic, and distress as I was harassed sexually and became a victim of sexual assault by a fellow platoon mate. I went through all of that alone because I never wanted to cause trouble for anyone. So I suffered in silence, endured the physical and emotional pain, and never told a soul. I know those things will forever be fibers in my being, but today I continue to live the life of a survivor. After such experiences, I continue my pursuit of happiness. I will persevere!

In fact, much of who I am today took a lot of personal and professional growth, prayers, and determination to do *the work* as it pertains to my healing. *The work* for me is intentional and effective efforts made toward a specific goal to bring about positive change in my life. In times like this, embrace yourself and make your efforts count. We will all persevere!

As a woman in the military, life was very rewarding yet complex and demanding to say the least. Having to juggle being a female Soldier, a mother, a former military spouse, and deal with separation from family due to permanent change of station (PCS) made things stressful at times. But I always thought that the life I chose would get better, and eventually it did as I found ways to balance it all. And yes, things will get better for you as well as you find or create your own sense of balance. You will persevere!

One of my most memorable times of stress was when I heard my child's screams echoing through the airport as I PCS'd (Permanent Change of Station), and the guilt I felt because of that. A one-year tour to South Korea turned into another dependent restricted tour to Kuwait, due to circumstances. That was when life shifted again tremendously for me as a Soldier. That same guilt I felt for leaving is something I have dealt with for many years as I wonder, "If I had not left, how would our lives be different?" Even though I know I made the best decision I could, my thoughts of "what if" remain. We are persevering!

I was never the same after Kuwait. I felt that was the one tour that took the laugh out of and away from me. I had never experienced such fear and uncertainty in my life as I did there.

All of us Soldiers received a briefing and I remember being told, "The next set of sirens you hear will not be a drill, but in fact the real deal."

Not long after that briefing, as a few of us ate in the dining facility, we noticed a news ticker at the bottom of the TV screen that stated, "Sirens Heard in Kuwait City." We looked at one another and said, "Sirens? What sirens?" We did not hear the sirens. Then, out of nowhere, the sirens blared through the dining facility as pure panic covered the entire room. The screams and the scramble of people, tables, and chairs brought about more chaos. More importantly, the fear in everyone's eyes was something I will never forget as we all seemed so unsure of what would follow the sirens.

Everyone helped one another out, as many seemed shaken and worried. Eventually, we bunkered under the tables. This was one incident of many that, again, changed me forever. I noticed that I would sit for extended periods of time and be somewhere else in my head while physically being in a place filled with people. I felt frozen, numb, and detached in so many ways but no one around me seemed to recognize that I was completely different.

It was very difficult some days, but because I had made it back home, I continued to push through the things I struggled with for the sake of my child. I sought out counseling because only I knew what I was dealing with deep down inside and the counseling helped me put things back into perspective. I persevered!

For the next few years after Kuwait and leading up to 2006, I struggled tremendously with things, some of which I did not have a name for until learning that it was post-traumatic stress disorder, depression, chronic fatigue, insomnia, anxiety, and even severe panic attacks. I struggled with weight gain as well.

I felt broken emotionally and sometimes I felt like a failure. Being confident was not enough, being a hard worker was not enough, being a great leader was not enough, especially when eventually it equated to whether you were perceived as fat or not. I spent years trying to make this right, but nothing seemed to work. So, I began yoyo dieting, but nothing seemed to work long-term. I knew how to work out, but my level of motivation was in the dumps, so I reacted by choosing an option that almost cost me my life. I got liposuction.

On March 8, 2006, I had liposuction which was a huge mistake for me! I was in the hospital overnight for recovery after my procedure and that is when everything went downhill. I formed blood clots everywhere. I could barely breathe and suddenly I blacked out. There were multiple pulmonary embolisms (PE), deep vein thrombosis (DVT), and according to the doctors, too many clots to count.

I remained in ICU for approximately 30 days, fighting to live. I was given an anticoagulant medication which was used to prevent the clots from getting larger and an inferior vena cava (IVC) filter was implanted to presumably prevent life-threatening pulmonary embolism. Later, it was decided that I should be medically boarded out of the Army. But my love for the Army and being a Soldier never diminished, so I fought for my career and was able to continue my active service until mission complete on October 31, 2012, as a Sergeant First Class with a retirement date of November 1, 2012. Giving me 20 years and 15 days active service. I persevered!

After meeting some amazing people through all of that, they and my family never wavered in my time of needed support. They prayed for me and they were there for me every step of the way. I thank them all.

Today, as a service-connected disabled American Veteran, I would never change my years of service for anything and I will continue to march through life's obstacles and live in my perseverance. Will you?

DIRTY LITTLE SECRET

☆ ☆ ☆ ☆ ☆

JACKELINE JOHNSON

Highly Functioning

Depression was my dirty little secret while serving on Active Duty. Have you heard the term highly functioning alcoholic? Well then, let me put it into context with my story. I would describe myself as a high functioning woman with major depression. Now keep in mind that this illness did not keep me from achieving my career goals in the Army. What she did do (yes, I do mean my depression) was help me lose friends and enter into volatile relationships and situations with men. My illness probably helped me to be successful in my career because of the aggressive nature of the military and what is perceived as a strength. I believe that being in leadership roles in the Army helped me to ignore the problem and helped my illness to grow immeasurably.

My first bout with depression was during my second permanent change of station (PCS).

The move was hard for me because my first assignment in the military had brought me back home where everything and everyone was familiar. I think that if I had been assigned to an unfamiliar place for my first military move this second move wouldn't have been so challenging. At the time I was in a relationship with a guy that did not deserve me. When I got orders to PCS, I tried to end the relationship because I had seen so many long-distance military relationships fail. This guy got on his knees and begged me to stay in the relationship. Thinking I was in love, I committed to having a long-distance relationship. All was well for about the first six months.

We managed to see each other two, sometimes three weekends per month and we spoke on the phone every night. However, I felt very alone in my new location and missed him, my friends, and my family like crazy. Here is where the depression that I thought was temporary started to rear her ugly head. After some time, I would call my so-called man and get no answer. Our visits dropped off and we started growing apart, but the more we grew apart the more I held on. I tried to hold on to that man as if my life depended on it. I started feeling insecure about the relationship; he said it was all in my head. Okay then, I played along with the "all in my head" crap until one weekend that I went to spend with him at his place. We were having a good time, but something was off, I could feel it.

I Saw Red

Night came, we were in bed asleep, and his phone rang. He answered the call and took the phone into the bathroom. Ladies, that was when I lost my shit! I banged on the door and tried to break it down, all while screaming, crying, and cursing. He came out of the bathroom and I punched him in the head. Well, I guess his momma never told him not to hit girls because he punched me back. Wow! We had a drag out fight and then the gun. He was a gun owner and I did the unthinkable. Yes, I grabbed the gun and pointed it at him. *What in the hell was I doing*! I could have lost everything—my career, my freedom, my family, and ultimately my life. I say my life because he wrestled the gun away from me and pointed it back at me.

During the heat of the moment anything could have happened. Again, you want to know what I was thinking? The answer is nothing, because an uncontrollable rage goes along with my depression and I can tell you that was one of the many times that I have literally seen the color red. Rage would consume my entire being and it was as if I wasn't present, but rather an innocent bystander watching the drama unfold. I wish that I could say that I walked away from the volatile relationship that this had become.

I did not.

We saw one another a few more times before I finally let it go. But when I did, my depression hit harder. It was so hard to function on a daily basis that I had to call my mom every morning before Physical Fitness Training or work call hours to talk it out, cry, and get it together enough to go to the office.

Competitive Nature

You would think that once I got to work that my performance would have been subpar, but it was not. I was and have always been driven in my professional endeavors. My family members and friends that do not know my struggle with depression will tell you that I accomplish anything that I set out to do. They are correct because the same depression traits that drove my rage also drove my competitive nature.

I excelled in my military career!

You see, because I was in a leadership position, I had subordinates (also known as employees). I would treat them harshly, yell, and take my anger out on them. Once I was in the office, I would put all of my energy into my tasks and it would help me forget the emptiness and loneliness that I felt inside. At work, I was perceived as reliable, productive, efficient, smart, and strong. Then I would go home and cry for hours, get in bed and do nothing, or eat my feelings away.

I did eventually seek the help of a psychiatrist and was diagnosed with a depressive episode. I wasn't honest with the doctor about all that was happening in my life. Why? Fear of reprisal from the military. If I had reported to a military doctor that I had been abusive and that at some point I had pulled a gun out on someone, they would have had to report it. There was no way that I was going to be honest with the doctor. The psychiatrist prescribed some anti-depressants. I felt better; I quit taking the meds and going to therapy. However, my depression didn't go away. It was always there keeping me company, at bay ready to come forth when she felt that I was in survival mode.

It was truly like having two personalities. The bouts of crying, not wanting to function, the rage, and the anxiety had become a crutch in some ways, and I did not want to stand up to her—depression. I did not want the stigma of having her, so I kept her as my dirty little secret for over 15 years. We had a secret affair for years. She helped me to ruin relationships with others which in turn helped to keep me isolated, just as she preferred.

No Longer a Secret

Fast forward to my retirement from the military. I decided to be a stay-at-home mom. This meant that I no longer had my subordinates or asshole peers to release the madness on, so I started channeling my madness unto my family. Until the day I saw this child looking back at me with fear in her eyes. Still, depression did not want to budge. I had to come clean about this secret relationship. I came clean with my husband and confessed all that I had been going through emotionally. See, he didn't know about my secret affair with depression. I kept her hidden from him for years. Oh, trust me, he knew something was wrong, but he thought I was just callous and complicated. He confessed that he thought of leaving on a few occasions. I had never let him in on the relationship because then I would have to let her go. Maybe I will one day write about how she was the second wife in my marriage. Ha! I was her comfort zone and she was mine. The relationship had gone on for so long, what would we do without one another?

The truth is that she is still with me and refuses to go away. However, we have agreed that she will no longer have a stronghold on my life and my relationships. Why? Because I no longer keep her as my dirty little secret. Our relationship is in the open now. I talk about her in counseling, I talk about her with my husband, I talk about her with my oldest child, I am talking about her to you. I also realized that I must take my medication to keep her in check because she is a disease. I am no longer ashamed of being on medication and the stigma that it carries. What I am ashamed of is that I let her control me for so long. What I regret are the ruined friendships and networks because of my refusal to deal with her poison. She seems to be a permanent part of me, but she no longer controls me nor does she define me, and I will never again succumb to her!

Many women in the military have a secret relationship with depression and are ashamed to deal with it because they don't want their chain of command to know, and they don't want it in their medical file for fear of the stigma. If this is you, learn from me and this story. Deal with your depression. Get the help that you need because if you do not get her in check she will spiral out of control and take you along for the ride. My advice to you is to find a safe place to get some help.

If I got a do-over, I would have continued with therapy, I would have stayed on the medication that was prescribed to me, and I would not have ruined special moments due to my dirty little secret relationship with depression.

If you have depression, there are many resources available to you. If you want to discuss how it is impacting your life or want to learn more about coping with depression daily, please feel free to contact me. I am more than happy to share more of my story on battling depression if it helps someone get the help that they need. Below are some resources if you need help battling your depression.

**International Foundation for Research
and Education on Depression**
http://www.ifred.org/

Depression and Bipolar Support Alliance (DBSA)
1-800-826-3632
http://www.dbsalliance.org/

National Institute of Mental Health
866-615-6464
www.nimh.nih.gov

American Psychiatric Association
703-907-7300
www.psychiatry.org/

Anxiety and Depression Association of America
240-485-1001
www.adaa.org

SOURCES

MEET THE
VISIONARY AUTHOR

LILA HOLLEY

Lila Holley is the visionary and founder of Camouflaged Sisters LLC, and uses multiple media platforms, programs, and live events to share the incredible stories of military women worldwide. Her award-winning, bestselling book series has been featured in The Huffington Post, Forbes, CBS affiliate news channel, and other media outlets.

Learn more at camouflagedsisters.org

MEET THE
COAUTHORS

CHARLOTTE CARROLL

Charlotte Carroll is the founder and director of Charlotte's Angels and partner with Texas Veterans Ranch and Family Resort (TVRAFR). Both are nonprofits, and one program is geared toward helping Veterans that suffer from PTSD (post-traumatic stress disorder) and TBI (traumatic brain injuries).

Charlotte is a Veteran herself that suffers with both PTSD and TBI. She battles with many challenges but uses her resources and experiences to help others. She is a retired state trooper and retired military Reserves; she served both her country and the State of Texas.

Charlotte is a mother of two girls, has one son-in-law, and is a grandmother. Her next project is a book that deals with suicidal situations and the families that are left behind. The proceeds from her books will benefit people with disadvantages, helping them overcome life's battles. Her passion for others is to be commended.

To connect, email her at charlotte.carroll53@gmail.com

ROLANDE SUMNER

Rolande Sumner is a retired US Army Veteran and the CEO and Founder of Life After Service Transitional Coaching LLC®. Rolande enlisted in the US Army National Guard in 1995 and retired in 2015. During her career she was an admin clerk, heavy vehicle operator, and human resources generalist/manager. She served as both a traditional National Guard Soldier and in an Active Guard/Reserve capacity. She's been stationed in Massachusetts, South Carolina, and Afghanistan. Today she is a case manager, military transition coach, and podcast host of *Life After Service Podcast*.

Rolande's passion is empowering and inspiring women Veterans to live full and authentic lives. Her mission is to dramatically empower Veterans to claim their autonomy, independence, and personal accountability through individualized mentorship, coaching, and training via the military transition to entrepreneurial process.

Learn more at www.facebook.com/pg/rolandessumner

AKIA CRUTCHFIELD

Akia Crutchfield (Bellona Oya) is the mother of two amazing children. She is a Sergeant First Class currently serving in the US Army. Akia has published a short poetry book titled, *The Petals of This Rose Are Not Easily Wilted*, in memory of her mother. Akia has also been featured in *Comes a Soldier's Whisper* by Jenny La Sala.

Having earned her bachelor of science degree in psychology, Akia is working on her master's in industrial and organizational psychology. Her goal is to be a servant leader and an inspiration to others.

Akia wants to be the voice of the unheard and the example to those who question whether they can make it out of the darkness or not. Prayers and good energy to those who turn the pages of this book.

To connect, email her at bellonaoya@gmail.com

NICOLE "COACH RED" REDMOND

Nicole "Coach Red" Redmond is her own boss at Redmond Legacy Coaching, LLC, the co-owner of Joyful Wealth Solutions, and the co-founder of M.A.D. About Your Business Organization. She is a mental health advocate, domestic abuse survivor, financial strategist, US Army Veteran, mother to a teen solopreneur, and a devoted wife. Her purpose is founded on a God-given revelation of three pillars: spiritual, mental, and financial. She serves these purposes through coaching, consulting, writing, community work, and spoken word.

She has co-authored *The Money Code and How to Crack It!* and *From Grief to Grind: The Journey of Denial, Acceptance, and Purpose.* She is currently working on her first self-published book of poems. She resides in central Texas and has a master's degree in psychology, a bachelors in information technology management, and is a certified debt and credit consultant and personal/business budget manager.

To connect, email her at Nicole.B.Redmond@gmail.com

BRANDY DAVIDSON

Brandy Davidson is a native of Carthage, Texas, and the mother of two beautiful children, Aysia and Alexander. She originally enlisted as a 63B, light-wheel vehicle mechanic but was able to gain experience in human resources and administration as well. Networking with others alongside the M.A.D. (Mindset, Accomplishment, Destiny) About Your Business crew as project coordinator is what motivates her. However, her passion is networking, planning, and organizing.

Not only does Brandy encourage others, but she has been encouraged by working and assisting at Teach Them To Love Outreach Ministries, a domestic violence shelter, as an administrative assistant. Any sports that her children attend, she selflessly volunteers her time as the team mom to help assist with putting out information.

Being in the military was a joy and she happily served 15 years in the US Army.

To connect, email her at brandyisoriginal@yahoo.com

TERESA JOY EDLOE

Teresa JOY Edloe was born in Baltimore, Maryland, but also considers herself a Texan as she lived in Texas for about 20 years. Teresa is now a retired military Veteran and retired federal agent for the US Air Force. Teresa holds a master's degree in criminal justice specializing in education towards anti-victimization. Teresa is passionate about helping others and works closely with a couple of non-profit organizations to combat hunger and homelessness and volunteers during local and national disaster relief efforts. Teresa also works with a non-profit to support their efforts in bridging the relationship between the community and law enforcement. Teresa is passionate about highlighting the importance of mental well-being and combating the stigmas related to mental health. She also enjoys using her life experiences, education, and training to help prevent patterns of victimization by providing self-defense, empowerment training, and educational resources to high-risk women and children.

To connect, email her at FindJOYnU@gmail.com

ELLA SMART

Ella Smart is the founder of Wise Woman Ministries where she helps to equip and encourage women and families. She is originally from Nigeria in West Africa. She is an aspiring author who is currently working on her first book.

Ella enjoys writing daily devotionals, motivational speeches, and poems and teaching Bible study at her Dallas home. She also blogs about her life experiences to encourage others and speaks at women's events. Ella is a minister of God who loves to pray and teach the Word of God. She has a degree in education and is currently pursuing her bachelor's in counseling while working as a school teacher.

Ella is a survivor of domestic violence and a thriving, whole solo parent of four children—Micah, Charis, Haven, and Joshua. She stands on the truth that "there are no hopeless situations, only a people who have lost hope."

To connect, email her at Elasticusa2002@yahoo.com

SANDRA G. ROBINSON

Sandra G. Robinson is a registered nurse (RN) with twenty-six years of experience and a tireless advocate for women Veterans. Her background has afforded her extensive familiarity with women Veterans' post-deployment issues and their gender-specific healthcare needs. Sandra served in the Army Reserve, 846th Transportation Company, from 1986-1992, serving overseas during Operation Desert Storm. She received numerous medals during her years of duty, to include the Southwest Asia Service Medal with three bronze Service Stars. While being deployed to war wasn't something she anticipated, the experience proved rewarding, leaving her with a profound sense of commitment to her sisters-in-arms. In 2017, Sandra founded Combat Female Veterans Families (CFVF) United. The purpose of CFVF is to encourage and facilitate positive reintegration experiences for combat female Veterans and their families through education, support, and advocacy. She serves as the organization's president.

To connect, email her at sandra.robinson@cfvfunited.com

ERICA WILKERSON

Erica Wilkerson is an empowerment coach and speaker focused on helping women and youth through self-care, creating vision and goals, and having a positive mindset and an accountability partner. She is a registered nurse who recently retired from the Army after 20 years of service. She has been working in women's health for the last 12 years.

Erica is dedicated to supporting and empowering women to improve their lives. She has played a key role in helping thousands of women change their lives for the better. Now she continues her mission to inspire, encourage, and motivate women to be the best version of themselves through her Perceptive Living business.

Erica's purpose is to ensure that women are taking care of themselves even as they take care of others.

Learn more at www.perceptivelivingnow.com

THERESA ALEXIS

Theresa Alexis, also known as The Military Bride Strategist™, is the founder and owner of Alexis & Crew Events, Design & Beyond. She is an educator, author, and speaker whose mission and purpose is to help couples, primarily military couples, cultivate their relationships by providing Beyond the Ceremony™ coaching. She also empowers women to live out their God-given purpose and activate their faith to new heights.

Born and raised in Birmingham, Alabama, Theresa Alexis joined the US Marine Corps right after high school, where she served for almost eight years. Theresa Alexis currently holds certifications in professional bridal consulting and Christian counseling and has been awarded with numerous letters of appreciation for her volunteering efforts. She currently resides in southern Mississippi with her husband and three children.

Learn more at www.theresaalexis.com

ROBIN LUDWIG

Robin Ludwig—author, poet, and closet Shakespearean—has been writing for over twenty years. Upon earning a B.A. in English from the University of Texas at Arlington, she taught literature and writing in Texas and in England. Since 2002, she has served in the US Air National Guard (ANG) and has volunteered for multiple humanitarian and hurricane response missions with the 136th. Medical Group.

Robin is passionate about Stephan Wolfert's De-Cruit course, a nonprofit program for Veterans that incorporates theater, Shakespeare, and science. In her spare time, she writes sonnets about her life in the military, homeschools her two sons, and travels the world with her race car driving husband.

Learn more at www.robinludwigwrites.com

VIOLET BRANTLEY

Violet Brantley is an Army Veteran and owner of The Salon Strategist Business Management Program. Due to her past successes and failures in the salon field, having practiced in the field for over 28 years, Violet developed a business management program designed to help salon owners bounce back stronger than ever. She believes that her program will strategically assist salon owners in maneuvering past, over, and through anything they will face as they run their successful business.

Violet has faced many life-altering experiences, but through the grace of God she survived and is fearlessly rising above her circumstances, speaking to encourage others that they too can never be defeated. She lives by the Scripture, Jeremiah 29:11 (KJV), "For I know the thoughts that I think toward you, saith the Lord, thoughts of peace, and not of evil, to give you an expected end."

To connect, email her at thesalonstrategist@yahoo.com

SHAYLA HAWKINS

Shayla Hawkins is a US Army Veteran with a passion to transfer vision so that others can see their purpose in life sooner rather than later. She currently travels the world providing support to Soldiers, Veterans, and their families. Shayla's passion was born at an early age as she was taught to always expect more and dream of better.

Shayla joined the military at age 17 and served for 14 years. During that time, she received a bachelor's degree in criminal justice from the University of Alabama at Birmingham. She also received her associate degree in theology from New Birth Bible Institute. Her love and desire to help people has been a key motivator to pursue a master's in counseling and human service. Shayla is the proud wife of Antonio Hawkins and mother of Jazmine and Anthony. She spends her leisure time with family, attending church and sporting events, and serving her community.

Learn more at www.hhbusinesssolutions.com

DONNA NEWMAN-ROBINSON

Donna Newman-Robinson is passionate about living her legacy every day. After retiring from her stellar career of 20 years serving in the US Army, she is now seen as one of the go-to motivational coaches for women Veterans who are in transition back to civilian life. Donna has been able to use her own personal and professional experiences as a US Army Nurse Corps officer to lead a successful career as a health care professional, business consultant, author, and certified professional coach.

Donna has been honored and recognized for her many accomplishments post retirement; however, she's most proud of her recent recognition as a 2017 AARP President's Award recipient for Community Service for her volunteer work with military Veterans. The experiences and challenges while serving gave her the inner strength to believe in her power and purpose, and to live her life on her own terms!

To connect, email her at donna@donnanewmanrobinson.com

JOYCE V. HAMILTON

Joyce V. Hamilton is from Brooklyn, New York, residing in Elizabethtown, Kentucky. She is an Army Retired Sergeant First Class who served in Iraq in 2003 and retired from working for the US Army Wounded Warrior Program (AW2) after a total of 34 years of federal service. She is the co-owner of The Lord's Supper Soup Kitchen Mobile Ministry, feeding the hungry and homeless in the community. Joyce is also a University of Louisville graduate with her bachelor and master of science in social work. Joyce is a missionary/evangelist and inspirational speaker for women who suffered from physical abuse and homeless. She is a professional advocate and change agent who has been featured in the *Fort Knox On Post Magazine, News Enterprise, Gold Standard, Turret, HCEC-TV Issues & Insights- Hardin County Schools*, and Army.mil stories. Together with her husband, Terriance (Army retired), they have five children and five grandchildren.

To connect, email her at joycehamilton030564@gmail.com

SHARON FINNEY

Sharon Finney is an Army Veteran on a mission to encourage and inspire, using writing, for growth and healing. She is the author of the memoir, *Sweet Magnolia*, and co-author of *Behind the Rank, Volume 1*, both of which are Amazon bestsellers. After publishing *Sweet Magnolia*, Sharon established the Magnolia M. Bradford Memorial Scholarship as a tribute to her late mother. Book sales helped to fund the first award in August 2018. Sharon's work has been featured in *Women Who Served* Magazine, the *Panama Cyberspace News*, *DIGEST THIS! Ministry Magazine*, and *The Pastor's Message*. She is a devoted wife and mother who enjoys spending time with her family and supporting charitable endeavors in her local community. Sharon and her husband, Lewis, are the owners of the metro DC consulting firm, L&S Enterprise, LLC, where they promote premarital counseling and marriage enrichment from a Christian perspective.

Learn more at www.LSEnterprise.org

SAMANTHA JEAN JASSO

Samantha Jean Jasso is 35 years old. She joined the Army as a Specialist at 27 years old (turned 28 in Basic Training). She holds a bachelor's degree in human development and family studies, which is about enhancing and improving the human condition, from Texas Tech University. Samantha served at Fort Drum for a little more than three years as a healthcare specialist.

After getting out of the Army, Samantha worked for the Veteran Resource Center (VRC) in Amarillo, Texas, as a VRC navigator for a year and four months. Since January of 2018, she has been an admin for the Veteran 2 Hire Facebook page. Samantha is also a certified peer specialist. Samantha's mission statement is "To help to not leave a comrade behind."

To connect, email her at samanthajasso@veteran.me

IASHA K. NICHOLS

Iasha K. Nichols always knew that she wanted to be a part of something that brought about new experiences and a sense of purpose in her life, so she set out to join the military from her hometown of Woodruff, South Carolina.

Her career began at Fort Leonard Wood, Missouri, and her Advanced Individual Training took place at Fort Gordon, Georgia. Iasha served a little over 20 years of active service in the US Army, from October 1992 until she retired in November 2012.

Iasha is currently pursuing her doctor of human services degree and has a master of science in human behavior while working as an equal opportunity compliance specialist for the Department of the Army. Iasha is married to retired US Marine Corps Gunnery Sergeant Bruce A. Nichols Jr. and has a beautiful daughter, Darasha D.M. Singleton.

To connect, email her at iashak.nichols@gmail.com

JACKELINE JOHNSON

Jackeline Johnson is a decorated retired Army Officer who served 21 honorable years. She is now a career and job search strategist, corporate trainer, and facilitator who is passionate about helping others. She is skilled at providing professionals with products, techniques, and resources to help them achieve their career and personal goals. Jackeline is committed to having a positive impact on those around her. She has developed and delivered training and coaching solutions at all levels of staff, utilizing the latest and most effective training and coaching techniques. In a meeting with her, you are guaranteed an energetic, committed, informed, and well-prepared coach/trainer.

Jackeline has a master's degree in management and leadership and is a dedicated wife, mother, and volunteer.

Learn more at www.linkedin.com/in/jackeline-johnson

1. TAKE A PHOTO

Take a pic of you with a Camouflaged Sisters book.

2. CAPTION IT

Tell us what you thought of the book.

3. TAG IT

INSTAGRAM

BOOK

REVIEW

Tag us @camouflagedsisters and Hashtag

#CamouflagedSisters

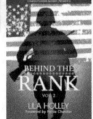

Visit us at
camouflagedsisters.org

CREATING DISTINCTIVE BOOKS
WITH INTENTIONAL RESULTS

We're a collaborative group of creative masterminds
with a mission to produce high-quality books to position
you for monumental success in the marketplace.

Our professional team of writers, editors, designers,
and marketing strategists work closely together to ensure
that every detail of your book is a clear representation
of the message in your writing.

Want to know more?
Write to us at info@publishyourgift.com
or call (888) 949-6228

Discover great books, exclusive offers, and more at
www.PublishYourGift.com

Connect with us on social media

@publishyourgift

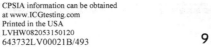